WRITING
MOTHERHOOD
A Creative Anthology

for all mothers

WRITING MOTHERHOOD

A Creative Anthology

EDITED BY **CAROLYN JESS-COOKE**

SEREN

Seren is the book imprint of
Poetry Wales Press Ltd,
57 Nolton Street, Bridgend, Wales, CF31 3AE
www.serenbooks.com

Introduction © Carolyn Jess-Cooke, 2017
Poems & Prose © individual authors

ISBN: 978-1-78172-376-0

A CIP record for this title is available from the British Library.

The publisher acknowledges the financial assistance of the
Welsh Books Council.

Printed by Short Run Press Ltd, Exeter

Cover Image: 'Mothers & Daughters, 2014' Oil on canvas
© Ishbel Myerscough

CONTENTS

9 Introduction

Transformations

21 Esther Morgan — This Strange New Life
26 Esther Morgan — Winter
27 Liz Berry — Connemara
29 Clare Pollard — The Reef
31 Anna Crowe — Amniotic
33 Nuala Ní Chonchúir — Die Schwangere
35 Mel Pryor — Emergency Birth
36 Christy Ducker — And
37 Doireann Ní Ghríofa — Postcards from a Hospital
39 Alicia Ostriker — Paragraphs
40 Alice Oswald — Poem for Carrying a Baby Out of Hospital
41 Natalya Anderson — The Woman in Clericals
42 Rebecca Goss — The Baby Who Understood Shadows
43 Sharon Olds — Interview with Sharon Olds on Motherhood and Writing
47 Sharon Olds — Her First Week

Slow Days, Fast Years

51 Clare Potter — Self-Soothing
52 Sasha Dugdale — Lifting the Bedcovers and There
53 Agnieszka Studzinska — Boat
54 Hilary Menos — White Pebble
55 Jacqueline Saphra — What Time is it in Nova Scotia?
56 Sinéad Morrissey — The Camera
59 Degna Stone — Ruby, Aged 4½
60 Rebecca Stonehill — Writer and Mother: How Children can help (and not Hinder) the Creative Process
63 Kate Hendry — Your Voice
64 Helen Dunmore — Domestic Poem
66 Carolyn Jess-Cooke — Hare
67 Rosie Sandler — Maternal Instincts
68 Deryn Rees-Jones — Afterthought
70 Rachel Zucker — The Day I Lost My Déjà Vu

Loss, Absence, Suffering

75 *Pippa Little*   For my miscarriage
76 *Nuala Ellwood*   The Weight of a Girl
78 *Catherine Graham*   Lullaby
79 *Becky Cherriman*   The Foster Mother's Blanket
80 *Wendy Pratt*   Sixth Birthday
81 *Kaddy Benyon*   Strange Fruit
82 *Geraldine Clarkson*   Monica's Overcoat of Flesh
83 *Elizabeth Barrett*   Good things happened on that day also
84 *Carrie Etter*   A Birthmother's Catechism
85 *Melissa Lee-Houghton*   Accident
86 *Marie Naughton*   Still
89 *Karen McCarthy Woolf*   Mothers' Day
91 *Karen McCarthy Woolf*   White Butterflies
92 *Jane Burn*   Only Child
93 *Julia Darling*   Advice for My Daughters

Mother's Work

97 *Anna Barker*   The 'Writer Me' and the 'Mother Me'
99 *Marianne Burton*   Meditation on the Hours: 5pm: The Lie of the Pool
100 *Hollie McNish*   31 May
103 *Rose Cook*   Poem for Someone Who is Juggling Her Life
104 *Ruth Stacey*   On the Cautious Road
105 *C.L. Taylor*   Motherhood Turned Me to Crime
107 *Janette Ayachi*   Plasticine Love Hearts
108 *Carrie Fountain*   Working Mother Poem
109 *Lily Dunn*   The Mutable Bed
111 *Tess Gallagher*   I Stop Writing the Poem
112 *Kate Bingham*   The World at One
113 *Sujata Bhatt*   29 April 1989
114 *Mary Austin Speaker*   After the First Child, the Second
116 *Zoë Brigley*   Motherhood *is* Valuable for the Creative Life
118 *Emma Donoghue*   Interview with Emma Donoghue on Motherhood and Writing

Mothers & Others

123 *Greta Stoddart*   At the School Gates
125 *Kathryn Maris*   School Run
126 *Louisa Adjoa Parker*   His Khaki Hood
127 *Stav Poleg*   At the Gallery of Modern Art
129 *Teika Bellamy*   Interview with Teika Bellamy on
                               Motherhood and Publishing
132 *Kathryn Simmonds*   Memorial
133 *Jo Young*   The Lady Standard-Bearer from the
                               British Legion
134 *Carol Ann Duffy*   Water
135 *Rachel Richardson*   Transmission
136 *Emma McKervey*   Patagonia
137 *Laura Kasischke*   Game
138 *Jackie Wills*   Giya's Maps
139 *Wendy Videlock*   Flowers
140 *Sarah Moss*   Interview with Sarah Moss on
                               Motherhood and Writing

Transitions

147 *Kate Long*   The Five Stages of Motherhood
151 *Julie Hogg*   Borrowing You Back
152 *Emma Simon*   Plait
153 *Jane McKie*   Archipelago
154 *Fiona Benson*   Eurofighter Typhoon
155 *Tina Chang*   Milk
157 *Deborah J. Bennett*   Laundry
158 *Rhian Edwards*   Parents' Evening
159 *Patricia Ace*   First Blood
161 *Natalie Shaw*   How to Tell Your Son He Has No
                              Friends
162 *Ellen Phethean*   Youngest Son Leaves Home
163 *Rita Ann Higgins*   Grandchildren
164 *Brenda Shaughnessy*   Magi
166 *Catherine Ayres*   Two Sons in a Lake
167 *Suzanna Fitzpatrick*   Fledglings

168 Notes on Contributors
185 Acknowledgements
188 Thanks
189 Editor Note

INTRODUCTION

There is no more sombre enemy of good art than the pram in the hall.
                                          – Cyril Connolly

T his book presents a selection of the most important contempo-
    rary writing by women on the tensions between motherhood
and writing.

Cyril Connolly wrote about the 'pram in the hall' in his 1938
book *Enemies of Promise*, yet his caveat is directed at men (he took
it as given that women create babies, not art). Nonetheless, the
quote is still in use to capture those devastating effects brought to
artistic creation by a new baby. I'm not alone when I admit the
arrival of my first child felt like stepping inside a whirlwind. I had
plenty to worry about – SIDS, whether she was gaining enough
weight, whether we could afford maternity leave, etc. – but I do
remember that among my worries was a serious concern that I
might never be able to write again. My brain felt completely
scrambled. I could barely construct a text message for weeks,
months. Time was disjointed. It seemed to take an inordinate
amount of time to do even the smallest task. I remember thinking,
over and over, *why did nobody tell me how hard this is?* After the birth
of my son, however, writing proved effective in pushing back the
darkness of postnatal depression, and also inspired a new direc-
tion in my creative practice; I had always thought I would only
ever write poetry, but the problem-solving, immersive elements of
narrative proved much more potent in batting back depression.
After the births of our third and fourth children, let's just say that
I became a bit more creative in how I managed my time.

PUBLISHING MOTHERHOOD

In 2014, Arts Council England funded my Writing Motherhood
project to tour literary festivals in the UK to discuss the impact of
motherhood on women's writing. I had read a number of reports
and articles that claimed the key to literary success was childless-
ness, or for a woman to have just one child, or at least to bear in
mind that each child 'costs' a female writer four books. None of
these reports aimed their caveats at men. I became curious – and

not a little dismayed – by the idealization of motherhood, and by the casual sexism that was prevalent and unchallenged in discourses about motherhood. I set up the Writing Motherhood project because I wanted to empower mothers and to encourage them to talk about their experiences. Although the assumption about mothers and writing was that we just didn't have the time or inclination (we're all too busy dealing with that pram in the hallway!), I perceived that other forces were at work, prohibiting women's writing from making it into the public sphere and/or being perceived as good literature. For instance, Pulitzer-prize winning poet Sharon Olds was famously rejected by a US literary magazine with the following note:

> This is a literary magazine. If you wish to write about this sort of subject, may we suggest the *Ladies' Home Journal*. The true subjects of poetry are ... male subjects, not your children.[1]

Olds' rejection occurred in the 1970s, and, as my interview with her on page 43 shows, she continued writing about her children, and with much success. But at our Writing Motherhood event at the 2015 StAnza Poetry Festival in St Andrews, Hollie McNish – a spoken word artist and published poet, whose poem 'Embarrassed' (about breastfeeding in public) went viral on YouTube in 2013, receiving over a million hits in less than a week – shared some exciting news: her new book, about motherhood, had finally been contracted for publication.[2] She added that the book had previously made it to three acquisitions meetings with other publishers, who had each turned it down for the same reason: motherhood was too difficult a topic to market. Like Sharon Olds and many others before her, McNish's dominating literary subject is the female experience (see page 100), and despite her huge following across social media, YouTube and throughout her solo UK tour, her work was deemed too 'niche' to publish. Let me repeat that: her subject, which referred to over half the human population, was too niche.

If McNish's experience does not suggest that the real obstruction to women's writing is the prevalence of sexism in mainstream publishing, then perhaps the following does. In 2014, *The Huffington Post* ran a piece by Sara Sheridan claiming that female writers 'earn averagely only 77.5% of what their male counterparts earn. That's taking into account the bestselling efforts of the likes of JK Rowling.'[3] In 2013 VIDA reported a vast discrepancy across British literary publications between female and male writers: *The Times Literary Supplement* published reviews of books by 313 female authors and 907 by male authors. Of those reviews, 297 were written by women and 726 by men.[4] In response to these statistics, *TLS* editor Peter Stothard stated that 'while women are heavy readers, we know they are heavy readers of *the kind of fiction that is not likely to be reviewed in the TLS'*.[5] What kind of fiction is that, exactly? In the same year, Alison Anderson's survey of publishing catalogues and literary prizes revealed that women's writing accounted for just 26% of works in translation.[6] That the publishing industry has historically patronized the female experience is a known fact (see my interview with publisher Teika Bellamy on page 129), but that it *continues* to fail to dismiss the female experience is shameful.

The Writing Motherhood project toured thirteen UK literary festivals with twenty female writers.[7] We came from a range of genres (poetry, spoken word, illustration/storytelling, journalism, fiction) and were all at different stages of raising children. Our discussions covered much more territory than I could have anticipated. We talked about the importance of supportive partners and friends, about why the project wasn't 'Writing Parenthood' but specifically about mothers, and whether the literature of motherhood was polarizing against women without children. Some participants talked about the occasionally toxic environment of playgroups and 'mummy mornings', with anxious, insecure mothers competing against each other, whilst others mentioned the 'sisterhood' they felt with other women after having a child. If ever there was evidence needed that, when we talk about motherhood in the West we are talking about class, identity, gender politics, and media discourse, this was it.

The prickly, political, heart-wrenching, leg-crossing and tender aspects of motherhood were picked over again and again during these events. What quickly became apparent during the tour was that the production of literature by women faced far more barriers than any pram in a hallway. For example, at our event at the Durham Book Festival in October 2014, bestselling novelist Kate Long discussed one of her books that portrayed some serious and sensitive issues, including the death of a child. Then she held up the book to our audience, revealing a pale pink cover with a cartoon caricature of a woman with a colander on her head – completely inappropriate for the book's tone and subject matter. Long's example was not a one-off: other participants and audience members spoke of books that had been packaged as fluffy, cute, and whimsical, even when dealing with serious subject matter, ostensibly to pitch the book at female readers.

The literary misrepresentation and/or patronization of motherhood in literature unavoidably affects women's writing as both practice and published literature. Motherhood ought to be celebrated and championed, and the pieces I present here speak to its many complexities with unflinching honesty. They capture both the tensions of being both a mother and a writer and the ways in which this duality can tap powerful creative energies (see Zoë Brigley's essay on page 116). Mothering can involve such long, lonely, voiceless days, and, for my part, writing became ever more urgent as a way of drawing energy, of speaking and bearing witness to marginalia and minutiae, a way of creating order out of chaos, and a way of walking back to myself. Writing remains an essential method by which to negotiate this new identity space. Tensions between mothering and writing still rise up, and I don't always write directly *about* my children or motherhood. As many of the pieces included here show, motherhood and writing can become integrated and mutually beneficial.

MOTHERHOOD AND WOMEN'S WORK

The question most frequently asked of the writers involved with Writing Motherhood was 'how do you find time to write?' It's a multi-faceted question. Most often people seemed to ask out of interest, and perhaps kindness, because in reality many women still do most, and sometimes all, of the childcare, housework, and general management of domestic affairs regardless of whether they work full-time, part-time or not at all. Says a report by the Overseas Development Institute, 'across 37 countries covering 20% of the global population, women typically undertake 75% of childcare responsibilities – with a range of from 63% (Sweden) to 93% (Ireland).'[8] Childcare is often prohibitively expensive, and although many countries in the developed world are updating employment policies to create a more appropriate work/life balance, women still carry much of the social, economic, and physiological burden of childcare and domestic duties. Astonishingly, maternity leave in the US – the world's sole superpower – is still not guaranteed, resulting in many American women returning to work long before they have made a full recovery from pregnancy and childbirth, and many disengaging from the workforce entirely.[9] Studies show that it takes twelve months to recover physically and mentally from childbirth, and longer where complications have occurred in delivery, yet a 2012 study found that one in four women in the US returned to work just *two weeks* after giving birth.[10]

I could take up a lot of space presenting research that lays bare the deleterious impact of inadequate maternity leave provision on women's health, and on the division of domestic labour in households around the globe, but suffice it to say that the message conveyed historically is that women's work is underpaid, invisible, undignified, worthless work. I would argue that this has influenced how women's writing is both perceived and published.

When it comes to writing, the question of 'finding time' relates to the act of writing as something a woman with kids shouldn't ordinarily set as a priority. Anne Tyler nods at this in her essay 'Still Just Writing', which iterates the question she was asked repeatedly: 'are you still just writing?'[11] Writing is frivolous, perhaps indulgent, subversive, and even selfish, when done by women, and serious and perfectly normal when done by men. It's the implication Connolly makes: the pram in the hall is attended by the female, not the male. He's the one doing the writing. Or rather, he's the one getting published.

Of course, there's another reason why people asked 'how do you find the time to write?': in recognition of the deep love that (usually) arrives with a new baby. I have cancelled events and holidays to be with my kids, let down friends and employers, am forever running late. Many women have joyfully given up hard-earned careers to raise their children. In her interview on page 43, Sharon Olds says, 'having children caused me to feel far more love than I had felt before.' Of course, this isn't just love for one's children. Friendships can become strengthened through motherhood, and many women help each other out precisely because they are aware of the magnitude of the task. Bestselling author Rosamund

Lupton, for instance, credits a group of friends with helping out with childcare when she was struggling to make a deadline for her first (appositely-titled) novel, *Sister*.[12] Often this assistance isn't anything to do with logistics but with emotional and creative support. Both writing and motherhood can be terribly lonely, isolated occupations, and the ability to speak openly with audiences and other writers about the nitty gritty of our profession during the Writing Motherhood tour created numerous bonding experiences and friendships that will stay with me for a long time. Sisterhood and friendship also informs the painting on the cover of this book, featuring Ishbel Myerscough (the artist), her daughter, and also Chantal Joffe and her daughter. Ishbel and Chantal are both artists and have supported each other throughout their careers. Says Myerscough, 'my friendship with Chantal has been very important to me and my work. We set out in the world together to be painters, our ambition was to paint and live from being painters.... We have been each other's constant.' Crucially, she adds: 'There is no jealousy or competition. We need to stick together to win. I enjoy all her successes and we feel free to be happy about our successes and equally our failures.'[13]

The ways in which women go about the work of motherhood is of keen interest to this book. As McNish's piece on page 100 makes clear, this work is often lonely, tedious, beautiful, excoriating, but none of these new tasks can be placed on a CV. There is probably no other female experience in which so many extremes are so often simultaneously present: sweetness and frustration, energy and exhaustion, smallness and magnificence.

MOTHERHOOD BY MOTHERS

Much work remains to be done to shift the literary subject from a predominantly male perspective. During the Writing Motherhood tour, we were asked repeatedly by audiences: how do we change this? The answer is attempted at in this book: the celebration of women's work, voices, experiences, and writing. In 1983 Alicia Ostriker's important essay 'A Wild Surmise: Motherhood and Poetry' took issue with the dominant view (as so boldly expressed in Olds' rejection note) that poetic subjectivity was male. Her counter-view is worth recounting at length:

The advantage of motherhood for a woman artist is that it puts her in immediate and inescapable contact with the sources of life, death, beauty, growth, corruption. [...] If the woman artist has been trained to believe that the activities of motherhood are trivial, tangential to main issues of life, irrelevant to the great themes of literature, she should untrain herself. The training is misogynist, it protects and perpetuates systems of thought and feeling which prefer violence and death to love and birth, and it is a lie.[14]

As a young mother struggling to find my way back to writing, that gorgeous, rare phrase, 'the advantage of motherhood for a woman artist', made me re-consider the relationship between motherhood and writing. The many ways in which this experience had drawn me deeper into the world, into compassion, and into the bones of existence, permeated my writing. The love I feel for my children sometimes feels almost dangerous, too much to be contained, and completely affects how I engage with the world as a writer. Like Alice Walker's 1976 essay 'A Writer Because of, Not in Spite of, Her Children' recounts Buchi Emecheta's novel *Second Class Citizen*, which is dedicated to her five children, 'without whose sweet background noises this book would not have been written',[15] my own children have played a key role in developing my creative process. The greatest surprise of all has been an echo of Walker's analysis of Emecheta: '[she] is a writer and a mother, and it is because she does both that she writes at all.'

Of course, this is not the case for every woman. Motherhood is not a rite of passage for female writers. We should never pit mothers against women who are child-free. The intention here is to re-think representations of and debates about motherhood vs. writing, and to champion literature that provokes a more honest and nuanced engagement with the female experience. The poems, essays, and interviews included here offer new ways of thinking about identity, memory, language, physicality, mortality, friendship, and love. They vocalize the conflict that often emerges between motherhood and writing, and show what happens as obstacles – both psychological and physical – are confronted. What follows is an insightful, diverse, witty and altogether timely effort to realize finally what Susan Rubin Suleiman aspired to over thirty years ago:

We know very little about the inner discourse of a mother; and as long as our own emphasis ... continues to be on the-mother-as-she-is-written rather than on the-mother-as-she-writes, we shall continue in our ignorance.... *It is time to let mothers have their word.*[16]

Carolyn Jess-Cooke

Notes

1. Quoted by Sam Scott, 'Alumna Sharon Olds wins Pulitzer for poetry', *Stanford News*, April 23, 2013. Available at: <http://news.stanford.edu/thedish/2013/04/23/alumna-sharon-olds-wins-pulizer-for-poetry/>.

2. Hollie McNish, *Nobody Told Me: Poetry and Parenthood* (Blackfriars, 2016) – an excerpt is on p. 100.

3. Sara Sheridan, 'Women Writers are getting a raw deal', *Huffington Post*, 25 April 2014. Available at: <http://www.huffingtonpost.co.uk/sara-sheridan/women-writers_b_5204437.html?just_reloaded=1>.

4. *TLS 2013 Vida Count*. Available at: <http://www.vidaweb.org/tls-2013-vida-count/>.

5. Benedicte Page, 'Research shows male writers still dominate books world', *The Guardian*, 4 Feb 2011. Available at: <https://www.theguardian.com/books/2011/feb/04/research-male-writers-dominate-books-world>.

6. Alison Anderson, 'Of Gatekeepers and Bedtime Stories: the ongoing struggle to make women's voices heard', *World Literature Today*, Nov 2016. Available at: <http://www.worldliteraturetoday.org/2016/november/gatekeepers-and-bedtime-stories-ongoing-struggle-make-womens-voices-heard>.

7. The writers were Carolyn Jess-Cooke, Kate Long, Kathryn Maris, Rowan Coleman, Sinéad Morrissey, Liz Fraser, Debi Gliori, Hollie McNish, Rebecca Goss, Helen Cadbury, Liz Rosenberg, Kathryn Simmonds, C.L. Taylor, Nuala Ellwood, Lily Dunn, Ruth Stacey, Mary Robinson, Steph Vidal-Hall, and Beverly Ward. The event toured the Belfast Book Festival, the Dylan Thomas Centre, the Dorothy Wordsworth Festival of Women's Poetry, Birmingham Literature Festival, York Literature Festival, Durham Book Festival, Hexham Book Festival, Swindon Festival of Literature, StAnza Poetry Festival, Wigtown Book Festival, Taunton Literature Festival, Ledbury Poetry Festival, and Off the Shelf Festival. See @writingmothers.

8. E. Samman, E. Presler-Marshall et al., 'Women's Work: mothers, children, and the global childcare crisis', *Overseas Development Institute* 2016. Available at: https://

www.odi.org/sites/odi.org.uk/files/odi-assets/publications-opinion-files/10333.pdf.

9. The Family Leave and Maternity Act entitles 'eligible' employees up to 12 weeks in a 12 month period of job-protected leave at no pay. See <https://www.dol.gov/whd/fmla/>.

10. Sharon Learner, 'The Real War on Families: why the u.s. needs paid leave now', *In These Times*, 18th August 2015. Available at: <http://inthesetimes.com /article /18151/the-real-war-on-families>.

11. Anne Tyler, 'Still Just Writing', in *The Writer on Her Work*, ed. Janet Stemburg (NY: Norton, 1980).

12. 'How novelist's friends helped her to top the book charts'. *Evening Standard*, Monday 27th Sept 2010. Available at <http://www.standard.co.uk/news/how-novelist-s-friends-helped-her-to-top-the-book-charts-6517998.html>.

13. By email, 30th Sept 2016.

14 Alicia Ostriker, *Writing Like a Woman* (Michigan: University of Michigan Press, 1983), p. 131.

15. Alice Walker, *In Search of Our Mothers' Gardens: Womanist Prose* (New York: Harcourt Inc, 1983).

16. Susan Rubin Suleimann, 'Writing and motherhood,' in *The M(o)ther Tongue: Essays in Feminist Psychoanalytic Interpretation*, eds, Shirley Nelson Garner, Claire Kahane and Madelon Sprengnether (Ithaca: Cornell UP, 1985), pp. 352-77 (352).

TRANSFORMATIONS

Esther Morgan

THIS STRANGE NEW LIFE

If I were writing this a year ago I would have known better what to say. I'd have been sharing with you a creative rhythm established over many years: the discipline of morning pages done in bed with a first cup of tea or on the bus to work, the importance of stopping and listening, the need to set aside longer periods throughout the year for sustained creative work. I'd have talked about the difficulties of finding windows of time for poetry when it's Windows that takes up most of our time. I'd have perhaps mapped out the journey of a typical poem for me – from initial inspiration through the, sometimes frustrating more often rewarding, process of editing to the final poem. In short I'd have had some advice to give.

*

It is four in the morning and I am trying to focus on the ornamental cherry framed by this window at the back of the house. It's high summer and the sky is just beginning to flush with light. I've been watching this cherry tree now night after night, day after day for over a month. I have tried to persuade myself that this bleary-eyed staring is akin to Buddhist practice. That there may be 13 or 20 or 100 ways of looking at a cherry tree. I try the odd mental haiku.

The tree remains obstinately separate. I can find no other words for leaves stirring, a blackbird arriving, the blue between the branches. In the time I've been staring, trying to notice something new, dawn has hardened into another day. My six-week-old daughter twists her head away to signify that she's replete, flinging her arms back in a milky swoon. I know I should wind her if we're not to have screams later, but I want to relish this stillness. The clock started ticking the moment the feed began: with luck I've got two hours and twenty minutes left. Say twenty minutes to wind and settle her back to sleep. Then two hours to crash before it all begins again. Suddenly seventeen syllables seems too long.

*

I used to write my poems during short sabbaticals from 'real' life. My creative practice involved a kind of stepping aside, like walking out into the garden at a party, the music and hubbub of voices suddenly beautiful because they are at one remove.

21

Moreover, this act of becoming adjacent has formed the subject matter of many of my poems. A lover of low roads and side chapels, guest rooms and ruins, the disused and deserted, I have sought in my work to capture pause, hiatus, those moments of rest in the complex score of living.

Now such moments, always infrequent, are becoming rarer. Even when my daughter's asleep it's hard to focus inwards, listening as I do for the first signs of her stirring. And with her arrival in the world I find I'm questioning my old poetic territory of solitude and silence. The unspoken fear, the thought I try hard not to admit into my consciousness, is that both my opportunity for writing and its source have been permanently displaced.

The sensation is like being swept out to sea on a lilo, only sitting up when it's too late to call for help. I can see the rows of tanned bodies and the bright parasols but I can't hear them flapping in the breeze, nor the children squealing as they run into the shallows. Somewhere on the rapidly receding beach is my little patch of sand, with its striped towel, its cairn of clothes and valuables.

*

Three months in and my days still revolve around her feeds. They come regularly like the offices of an enclosed order – Matins, Lauds, Terce, Prime, Sext, Vespers, Compline. Is the analogy so fanciful? Like the nun or monk's devotions the rhythm of caring for a newborn continues whether you want it to or not. Most things in life I've had a choice about – this one I don't. The structure exists – relentless and beautiful, boring and tender – however you feel about it. In a spare moment I Google monastic life. I learn that the purpose of morning prayer or Lauds is praise and that of Evening Prayer or Vespers is thanksgiving. Rhythm, structure, praise, thanksgiving. I feel I'm being taught something if only I weren't too blitzed by tiredness to take it in.

*

Some mornings, very early, I trundle my daughter up the lane in her red buggy, to get her to sleep after her dawn feed. She lies with her head turned to one side, her eyelids shadowed blue and almost translucent, as if dreaming of whatever star she's fallen from. The air, chilly with a heavy dew coupled with the physical effort, gets my blood flowing. I find myself wanting to identify the wildflowers we pass along the way. I want to know more intimately this

22

small world on my doorstep, the world I used to speed by in the car. Already its landmarks are assuming the significance of folk tale – the dead oak, rooks' wood, the far field where we always turn for home. Places that, perhaps one day, she will make up stories about. Gradually the litany of names grows longer, the blur of green coming into focus: yarrow, groundsel, doves-foot cranes-bill, wild mallow.

*

Everything goes into the mouth – keys, building blocks, cardboard boxes, spoons, rattles, soft toys, hard toys, things that should and things that shouldn't. It's as if the world doesn't exist unless it's tasted. Hers is a hand-to-mouth existence – for five minutes at a time she is utterly absorbed in the silkiness of a ribbon or the crunch of a window envelope. Simple and unlikely objects are utterly entrancing – the care labels on a teddy, the springiness of a whisk. Each day I kneel like a permanent wise man in front of my baby offering up sounds and sensations for her delight.

On good days I can accompany her on this exploration. I can abandon the will to do anything else other than be with her in the moment. On good days I too can be satisfied by the weight of a pebble in the hand. On good days we sit happily banging building blocks together like stone-age toolmakers. Around six months it occurs to me I haven't sung this much since I was a child.

*

Then there are the bad days. Days when I wake with a knot of nerves in my stomach that I can't unpick. Days when Larkin's line about new mothers comes back to haunt me: 'Something is pushing them/ To the side of their own lives.' Days when we're the only passengers on the mid-morning bus as it sways through empty villages like a lonely elephant. Days when I can't submit willingly to the usual routine, when I chafe and fret, unable to focus on what she is experiencing, the only thoughts in my head about all the other things I could, and would rather be, doing. The idea of writing a poem seems light years away, my imagination desultory as a market town on half day closing.

It's on days like these I think – darkly, unfairly – that if I were a male poet or a wealthy poet or a young poet I'd have the time and energy to write about my baby with all the enchantment of a new lover. I'd have thought of twenty similes by now for the way her eyes have changed colour from slate blue to hazel. I'd be comparing her to the sea and the moon in some kind of extended metaphor for gravity and love.

It's five o'clock and there's nothing left to play with, I'm trying to leave the room without her screaming, she's got no clean sleep suit for the night, the bottles need sterilizing, I have a streak of crusty sick down my jumper which I've probably been wearing all day and the wheels on the bus are *still* going round...

*

Writing begins again in the smallest of ways, with the attempt to note down each day one thing to be thankful for. I worry this is sanctimonious, perhaps it is, but it helps – to take stock, to find a space that allows me to set aside doubt, fear, tiredness. And even on the toughest days it's cheering that, when I think about it, there's something to record – a phone call from a friend that lifted the spirits, the courtesy of the elderly couple who smiled and stepped aside for us on the narrow pavement, my daughter's squeak of excitement as I helped her lift the flaps of a favourite book. These fragments retrieved from each day are not much in themselves. They are certainly not the start of some grand new poetic project but together they are helping to shift something. It does me good each night to see them on the page, words persisting, pushing their way through the odd crack in this strange new life.

*

We have made it to Christmas. Happiness is wrapping paper and a gold curly ribbon. Outside, bulbs are waiting in the ground for the year to tip again towards light. Poems like the earliest flowers are also beginning to stir.

What I am learning, what my daughter is teaching me, is that I need to try to find poems in the music as well as the silence. That by entering as wholly as I can her world of discovery, my writing might become a part of the rhythm of living rather than apart from it. I know that to get the writing done will still require solitary time, but I'm beginning to hope that what comes out of that is a poetry of connection rather than escape.

A poem I read recently by Jaan Kaplinski, 'The washing never gets done', has come to mean a lot to me. It's a poem about the muddle of domestic existence but it ends on a moment of attention: 'The wonder is that beside all this one can notice / the spring which is so full of everything / continuing in all directions – into

24

evening clouds, / into the redwing's song and into every / drop of dew on every blade of grass in the meadow, / as far as the eye can see, into the dusk.'

As the new year gets underway my hope is that I can make good on the possibility this poem holds out – that a creative life and a daily life can co-exist, that perhaps, over time, they can become the same thing.

*

If I were writing this a year ago I would be aiming for completion and symmetry, the satisfying clunk click of a safety belt. But that's not how life is at the moment. Rhythm, yes, but completion no.

So I am going to button my daughter into her rainbow striped fleece and head out the door. It's the first day of spring. Although there have been days this winter as mild, there is in the air that indefinable thrill that makes people pause on their doorstep and breathe in the change. Something about the volume of birdsong, the great fluttering and chittering in the hedgerow, the faintest greening along the branches of the trees, the spears of the early bulbs pushing through the leaf litter which, never mind, I didn't get around to raking up. The sound of a biplane from the nearby airfield is like a message from a summer sky. By then she'll be a whole year old. Meanwhile we have a bus to catch, something to see for the very first time.

Esther Morgan

WINTER

Sometimes when you're not with me
I wish I missed you more.

This morning I handed you over to the girl
who offered you the same sweet smile as all her charges

who led you away along the brightly painted corridor
as you looked back at me roaring *No!*

What kind of a mother am I to weigh these words
against your distress?

These being all I have to show for the hours I left you
except for the owl I might have otherwise missed,

gliding silently through the daylight garden
with her soft feathers and merciless gaze.

Liz Berry

CONNEMARA

I stepped out of my skin
that dusk in Connemara
where bush crickets thrummed
like pylons
and the lane smelled
of tar and clover.
What lay beneath
was fragile, not yet
ready for its season.
The drizzle
made sore music
of my nerve endings.
I was beautiful to the crows
as a butcher's window.

In the dusk, I was glorious,
so raw I felt each mote.
Kites beheld
my glowing jellyfish brain.
My heart was carmine,
radiant as a saint
in a wayside shrine.
I raised my arms
to the sky
and the air kissed me
with its stinging
worshipful mouth.

I threw the skin to the wind,
that sweet sack
I had tended and punished
for thirty-three years.
Now moths would make
heaven of it.
Let them come,
I thought,

I am ready;
for inside me you pulsed,
single celled,
extraordinary.

Clare Pollard

THE REEF

Pregnant already, I launch
my body into the Red Sea.
Cleavage, differentiation.
The mask lets in a slosh and
salt sears nostrils as I gasp,
dip, hook eyefuls of black
or cabbage, slopes of fire,
lion, parrot and angel, sard-
-ines flickering like lashes
against glare, bleach blue,
barred butterflies, a sea-
star in the Japanese garden's
surgical green, octopus fuss
over fronds, reticulate gold.
Implantation, zona hatching.
I listen to the earfuls of
wet heart, amongst polyps,
veinwebs, worm, thicklip,
feet kicking, wounding
coral that loosens its pink
gametes to snowstorm up
like winter's opposite like
the human embryo, merry
clownfish, still gill-slitted,
swishing in me later as I
unwrap the guide to tropical
fish, a birthday gift, travel
pornography as freedoms
dissolve or ebb from me,
who once raced reef sharks
with women in burqinis,
who was once chased for
white meat through black
and fan by men's lust
to touch a mythical beast.
Small sulcus or groove

forms above eye and below.
I paddle through pages,
dip, see squishy skulls
of moon jellies breathing
like ultrasounds, phantom,
flatworm, fringe, sourcream
scales, cowrie, clitoral
fingerlings, moray's startle
of eyes locked in fear at her
own mouth, needles, violet
rhinophores, moonsnail
drag of mantleskirt, kimono,
the ray a loose shadow,
speckle, puffer and lavender
in the unimaginable water,
simmering and acidified
in this translucent second
but still so full of world that
a flung face can shatter
a palest turquoise rinsing
through to skyfuls of sun.

Anna Crowe

AMNIOTIC

for Christopher

Far out in childhood's blue bay
the mast of the *John Egan Lane*
leaned like a pen in an inkwell;

in summer the willow-pattern china
on the black, worm-eaten Welsh dresser
shrugged off light dealt by the sea.

Months before you were born
you were already trying to hurl yourself
free of the water like a salmon,

and in the old delft-tiled bathroom—
Edwardian country-house turned hospital—
seven months gone, I lay and watched

a wherry's sails waver
in warm water, as children skated,
bowled hoops and played at hopscotch.

While women drew water from a well, or churned
butter, their men-folk fished from dykes, walked
on stilts or followed a plough;

keeping time with ancient plumbing,
windmills on either hand creaked and juddered
and my belly rose above the water

like a small polder. With so much
dedicated labour all around,
I almost believed that when you surfaced

you'd bring my childhood wreck
bubbling up from the sea-bed,
and that the old dresser would rise

with its load of dripping delft. But
by then you were already intent
on your next project, of fathoming the world.

Nuala Ní Chonchúir

DIE SCHWANGERE

~ pregnant in Karlsruhe ~

The other poets drink damson schnapps
from thistle-head glasses.

My baby flicker-kicks
with all five ounces of her weight,
with all four inches of her length.

I dream her hand
pipping from the egg of my belly
like a wing through shell,
I hold her embryonic fingers,
thrilling at her light touch.

Delighting in my blooming belly,
I feel my nestled passenger,
she flicks and settles, settles and kicks;
her cells gather, graceful as an origami swan
in perfect folds and re-folds.

In perfect folds and re-folds
her cells gather, graceful as an origami swan
she flicks and settles, settles and kicks;
I feel my nestled passenger
delighting in my blooming belly.

Thrilling at her light touch
I hold her embryonic fingers,
like a wing through shell,
pipping from the egg of my belly,
I dream her hand.

With all four inches of her length,
with all five ounces of her weight,
my baby flicker-kicks.
From thistle-head glasses
the other poets drink damson schnapps.

Mel Pryor

EMERGENCY BIRTH

A cut like a needle's eye
and he's through – a boy! –
a five pound four ounce ravel of son
asserting breath, but holding on

by just the skin of his gums,
the small resolve of vernixed lungs
whispering *Yes* as his skin is a swab,
his throat a hole, a plastic tube.

Later she eavesdrops at his mouth
for life. Her T-shirt blots two clouds
as nearness spills her eager milk.
They say it'll take a miracle.

Inside her a kind of god-love lifts –
breathe, baby, keep breathing, live.

Christy Ducker

AND

suddenly you are here
and I am astonished
by the way you smell of bloody bread
and the way you already decide
to place a webbed hand here,
to slow-wink a newt's eye there.
I am astonished that you are purple.

And now I know glee
at the indignant heaving bellows of your belly,
your self-startled arms flung wide proclaiming
your tiny chimp gums.

And I watch to see time
measured by your face,
crane as you push each new word through glottal air.
I thrill because you're not like me
but you and young and other.

Doireann Ní Ghríofa

POSTCARDS FROM A HOSPITAL

The afternoon that I walk through the hospital doors, I walk away from a poem in which I've grown a forest. I imagine the laptop cursor blinking in my absence until the screen darkens. In the emergency room, a long scroll unravels from a machine bound to me. I find some paper and scribble notes, the curve and dot of question marks. When a nurse pushes a syringe under my skin, I turn my head toward the window, my eye raking the horizon in search of a tree.

~   ~   ~

I lie in surgical theatre, naked from the breast down. Spinal morphine lifts me. Fourteen people in blue gowns and masks work on my body. I watch my daughter's birth. She is the tiniest baby I have ever seen. Outside, a sapling bends towards the window and watches too.

~   ~   ~

Minus one: my daughter is taken to the basement of the building, the Neonatal Intensive Care Unit. I lie on floor three, restrained by drips, catheter, and cannula, livid with my anaesthetised legs. I fret that she is waking up alone, blinking in my absence. On the line between land and sky, trees wave to me, leaves fluttering green and lush at the end of each twig. Branch begins to rhyme with distance.

~   ~   ~

In a wheelchair, I am brought to my daughter's side. She lies in an incubator, surrounded by strangers and wires. Her skin is pale, luminous, translucent. A bruise blackens on one tiny hand, where blood was drawn to be sent abroad. Under the shadow, blue veins branch and splay. The word I hear most these days is blood — Blood blood — Blood blood — a steady thud that reverberates in my head like a pulse. Holding her in my arms, I remember diagrams I learned for long-ago exams, the arterial tree, its vessels branching and splitting from the heart outward.

~ ~ ~

I sit on a single hard plastic chair under a fluorescent light and
stare at my tiny daughter. She lies very still. She will not feed. She
will not wake. We are moved to the acute area, where her incuba-
tor sits by a glass door: EMERGENCY EXIT. Every hour I descend
to the basement in search of my Persephone. I scrub my hands and
arms again and again with oily red surgical soap. I sit by the incu-
bator and cry. My skin turns scaly and raw. My eyes grow red,
then dry. I cry. I laugh. I cry.

~ ~ ~

Weeks pass. The nurses tell me that my daughter looks like me. I
doubt them as I peer at my reflection in the toilet mirror, but in her
incubator she too is dark-haired, pale, trembling. She lies very still
among wires and tubes. When she opens her eyes, I remember the
mirror at the heart of Francis Bacon's studio. In that wilderness of
brushes, tins, paint, easels and slashed canvases, a single circular
mirror slants against a far wall — glass eye, a calm reflection of
commotion. Her eye, when it opens, is dark as a mirror at night,
drinking from the muddle and movement of the ward. Her eye,
when it opens, seeks me out like a mouth.

~ ~ ~

Alicia Ostriker

PARAGRAPHS

If you look at a mother with a newborn infant, you see not two animals but one. They are placed in a kind of trance together, so that even when separated, a fleecy mesh connects them. The mother seems sleepy. She acts in a dream. She has little conversation, but shines at people, and wants to show them the baby, soft in its soft clothes and blankets. We see this also among the great sociable apes: when a new chimpanzee is born, the mother shyly exhibits it. Females, males, even dominant males, as well as older juveniles, come by to look and fondle it.

That fondling, touching-activity, vocalization: these are to teach, they rise from the forest like birds, so that beyond the sleeping, crying, feeding, shared by the mother and child, is pride of accomplishment. It kicks, it waves wild arms, it holds its head up on its stem. It will roll over, crawl, grow teeth. At the same time, anger. This is a prison. It exhausts the sap, the very juice. It does nothing but open its mouth. Can she never regain her autonomous self, her sunny wind-drenched leaves? She wants to kick – get off me, parasite. To kill it. To go mad.

All that is weak invites the brute. If I fail to acknowledge my will
to murder the child, to wipe him like spill from a counter –
then all that I call my love will evaporate, will choke.

When the mists lift, there are images. What the mother sees is the divine infant, showing where they come from, Eros, Jesus, Krishna, Blake's boy on the cloud commanding song. What does the child see, when he smiles at her as if he would be happy forever? As in the chapel ceiling, in the creation: the aged and youthful heroic figures recline amid clouds, their forefingers just parted. Michelangelo as an artist would have known: that which was once within you, life of life, you create in freedom. You release it, you open your hand, you let it go. In a few weeks that particular smile will pass, from the mother, to the father, to others.

Alice Oswald

POEM FOR CARRYING A BABY OUT OF HOSPITAL

like glass, concealed but not lost in light,
has structured into it a stress
that will burst out
suddenly in a shock of cracks, it's all
a matter of terror to hold right
what has a will to fall
and water for instance has the same weakness

the way the level ends of stockstill water break
at the touch of a raindrip, it demands
that kind of calm to walk
with a wafer of glass which if you slip could sheer
straight through a foot or neck
o infinite fear
entirely occupied upon two hands

and even a cobalt blue ingot of glass,
if you think of it, purpose-built
to be melted away, its mass
has an effect which makes it light
it moves through light to the heart of emptiness
though a slight
tap on its surface opens its integral fault

Natalya Anderson

THE WOMAN IN CLERICALS

In the hollow of my mother's bed,
on flannel sheets she sprinkled with freesia-
scented talc, she rolls onto her side, leaves

an impression of warmth. I burrow
into her dented cocoon, reach out for her
body, listening for the rasp

of St Francis of Assisi carved with heavenly
creatures, dragging along her thick silver chain.
It stops, wedges between her breasts

to announce that she is rising. I follow,
disciplined by the sudden cold; fold
the sheets back over her creases. All day

I wait, thinking about her warm palms
underneath my toes, thumbs and fingers
wrapped around to meet each other.

Rebecca Goss

THE BABY WHO UNDERSTOOD SHADOWS

She found him, on his front, one arm raised
and conducting the air. Three months old,

his limbs mere feelers on her carpeted home,
until the sun tipped his shadow on the floor:

made a shape impossible to push or pull
and he acted upon it. She believed

he was reaching, that his fingers
wanted to grab, but the shadow

was all there was, dancing
beneath his elbow. He hadn't heard her

come into the room, hadn't flexed
to her milky scent. She watched

as the link between light, object, surface
became coherent to this speechless being.

His eyes followed fist. The fist she held
in her lips, when love required her to eat him,

in mouthfuls. This baby she washed, fed,
kept close as fog, now able to see through

the branches of her arms, find the sun's rays,
his own shadow, all things that are not her.

INTERVIEW WITH SHARON OLDS ON MOTHERHOOD AND WRITING

September 2016

Carolyn Jess-Cooke: You didn't start writing poetry until you had children, did you?

Sharon Olds: I wrote poems and stories – and drew, and danced, and sang, and played with sticks and rocks in creeks, and played with dolls – when I was a child, and kept doing most of these as an adolescent and young adult. And one day, about two weeks after I turned 30, poems started coming to me almost every day.

What had happened the day before was not that I'd had children – they were about 2¾ and 9 months – but that I had received my Ph.D. degree (which had taken me eight years), and I would never have to take a test again.

I had gone with my kids to pick up my diploma – to the very plaza at Columbia University where, in May, 1968, undergraduates had occupied a few of the buildings, and some of us graduate students had spent a night sleeping on the sidewalk in support of them.

The statues, the stairs, the gates, were for me still saturated with that atmosphere of patriarchy questioned, and racism and sexism questioned – a scene of rebellion, non-violent protest, and violent official reaction to that protest.

Resistance remained in the stones and bricks and bronze. And when the poems started arriving, started occuring to me, the next day, they were poems of resistance and praise.

(Three poems of mine in which these experiences are embodied come to mind: p. 'May, 1968', *The Wellspring*, Knopf (US), 1995, Jonathan Cape (UK), 1996; 'The Defense', *Blood, Tin, Straw*, Knopf, 1999, Jonathan Cape, 2000; and 'Faust, 1972', (*Plume Poetry*, 2012.)

Carolyn: How would you say motherhood affected your writing?

Sharon: I would say that having children caused me to feel far more love than I had felt before. It opened my heart and mind and senses to the beauty and reality of our species at its youngest – and the beauty and reality and magic of reproduction. It gave me time to observe, and cherish, and serve. It gave me things to do which I knew were valuable, and I knew a lot of people thought of them as not valuable. It gave me the presence, and gradual partial knowledge, of two extraordinary people. It gave their father and me a source of delight, and learning, and co-operation. And it gave me stories, and portraits – 'subjects' – songs. It inspired and moved me to my soul and below, to my animal soul.

Carolyn: Did motherhood bring challenges to your writing?

Sharon: I would say my writing brought challenges to my children. How weird is it for some version of oneself to be leading its strange 'life' out in the world in a work of art written by one's parent? In the early days, I sort of thought no one would ever read the poems which were pouring out of me. I used my kids' names (later I went back through the books and in subsequent printings took the names out); I didn't have a good sense of discretion or courtesy. Later, when one of them asked me to stop publishing new poems about them, I agreed – later still, I would ask their permission before a poem went out, and they could take out anything they were uncomfortable with – or take out the whole poem. I think this has worked O.K. I have a better sense now of their privacy. And poems inspired by them in the past couple of decades – there are folders those poems go in. They're not shocking poems – just (in my case, in my opinion) intrusive. They can wait to be read.

Carolyn: One of the things that struck me as a new mother (9 years ago!) was the new language that accompanied this experience. Words like 'meconium' and 'mastitis' and phrases like 'let-down' were either unknown to me or took on an utterly different meaning.

Sharon: Yes! The vocabulary! Yum! Yay!! Brave new worlds of words have been entering poetry in the past twenty or thirty years – language of parenting, of sex, gender, race, class – a more complete set of references and musics!

Carolyn: Your poems 'The Clasp' and 'Looking at Them Asleep' resonated so deeply with my own experience that poetry became an integral part of experiencing motherhood, of attempting to define and understand it. Do you think your motherhood triggered a similar shift in reading and/or engaging with language?

Sharon: I had what for me was the great good fortune of our being able to afford my being a 'full-time mother'.

I had a lot of questions about mothering. I needed to experience it, to find out about it. What was it? What did the bond feel like? What was good-enough mothering? How different a family could I build from the one I'd been born into?

Our kids were born in 1969 and 1972. At the playground, on West 97th Street and Riverside Drive (New York City), around the sandbox, I met other young and youngish mothers and fathers. There was a fresh new wave of feminist consciousness in the air – though most couples I knew then were in the old-fashioned family roles.

I think the level of imagination in the gender dialogue these days is higher than it was then, and the discourse more intimate. I did feel some solitude and challenge in my strong ambition to write as well as I could (or a little better!), whatever that would mean.

But I think my relative isolation in the beginning helped me, too. I was writing, without being quite aware of it, in 4-beat lines – each line having 4 strong (accented) syllables and any number of unaccented ones. And when I came to what felt like the rhythmic end of a line I wanted no rhyme, no comma, no pause, but to ride right over and loop down and around to the left, to the beginning of the next line – to enjamb – consistently – to sail out into the blank space of the page, spiraling down to make a kind of whirling dervish shape. And I could do this! No one was watching me.

So I might add to the end of the question above: ('Do I think the circumstances of my writing triggered a shift in reading and/or engaging with language and with meter?') Yes.

Carolyn: The idea of 'the pram in the hallway' (sadly) still seems relevant for female artists; indeed, the most common question I'm asked as a writer is 'how do you find time to write'? It's a question male writers with children just don't get asked. Was it something you were asked? How did you respond?
Sharon: But don't you think it would be true now that if a doctor were married to a writer, and they had small children, and the doctor was a woman, and the writer was a man, that the man might get asked that?

Carolyn: What's interesting about the question 'how do you find time to write?' or 'how do you do it?' is that, between mothers, it's a question filled with intrigue. Many of us do struggle, particularly in the early years, to find headspace and/or time to create. Sylvia Plath's routine was between 4am and 6am, before her children got up for the day. I used to write poems in the bath. Did you have a particular writing routine when your children were small? Did that change?
Sharon: Nap time. Then a couple of years later, play-group! Then nursery school mornings – then the new baby's nap fitted into the nursery school

morning. Eventually, two simultaneous full school days.

And if an at-home parent has a partner who goes to work M-F, 7-7, the home parent might have Saturdays – dawn to 2, say – to write!

And as they got old enough I would sometimes be writing (or typing or revising) after I had picked them up from school. I'd be drinking tea, and if they needed me (not urgent – urgent was immediate) I'd say, 'When I'm done with this cup,' and they'd come in and check my cup – they'd look at 'the tea clock.' (It was important for me to play fair! To not push what the market could bear.)

Carolyn: What quickly became apparent during the Writing Motherhood tour was that the production of literature by women and/or about the female experience, motherhood included, faced far more barriers than any pram in a hallway. Your early work faced some rejection by magazines who claimed that the true subjects of poetry are... "male subjects, not 'your children'." Do you think publishing has moved on? Is the dominant perspective in poetry still a male one?

Sharon: I think the quote was, 'This is a literary magazine. If you wish to write about this sort of subject, may we suggest the *Ladies' Home Journal*. The true subjects of poetry are ... male subjects, not your children.'

On another printed literary magazine rejection slip was hand-written, 'Sharon Olds, Eat my razor'. This shocked me and did not shock me. What woman has not sensed it out there, the hatred of women? If we're lucky, we also experience the love of women – our own love of women, and others' love of women too..

Carolyn: Have you any advice for other women writing about motherhood?

Sharon: I think art is as old as our species, and arose out of our need to praise, and mourn, and to know ourselves and each other. Someone who has knowledge of a subject like motherhood, which through most of human history had not been memorialized or embodied in art, has precious knowledge. I think it's a matter of our survival and the earth's survival for us to get to know ourselves as quickly and deeply as we can.

Otherwise, my advice would probably be the same as the suggestions I make to any young writer. Take your vitamins. Exercise. Don't drink too much. Dance! Sing! Take care of your instrument – your body and mind. Protect yourself. Find a way to love yourself. Talk kindly to yourself! As often as possible, kiss your wrist. Kiss your wrist with feeling.

Sharon Olds

HER FIRST WEEK

She was so small I would scan the crib a half-second
to find her, face-down in a corner, limp
as something gently flung down, or fallen
from some sky an inch above the mattress. I would
tuck her arm along her side
and slowly turn her over. She would tumble
over part by part, like a load
of damp laundry, in the dryer, I'd slip
a hand in, under her neck,
slide the other under her back,
and evenly lift her up. Her little bottom
sat in my palm, her chest contained
the puckered, moire sacs, and her neck –
I was afraid of her neck, once I almost
thought I heard it quietly snap,
I looked at her and she swivelled her slate
eyes and looked at me. It was in
my care, the creature of her spine, like the first
chordate, as if the history
of the vertebrate had been placed in my hands.
Every time I checked, she was still
with us – someday, there would be a human
race. I could not see it in her eyes,
but when I fed her, gathered her
like a loose bouquet to my side and offered
the breast, greyish-white, and struck with
minuscule scars like creeks in sunlight, I
felt she was serious, I believed she was willing to stay.

SLOW DAYS, FAST YEARS

Clare Potter

SELF-SOOTHING

After you have screamed the roof off, pleaded
that you 'need the boogers out,' that 'my baddie
is hurting,' that you want
Auntie Sharon, not me,
and that you 'don't like the ni-night!'

I leave you to it because a poem wants
writing and I can't lose it to you.

You don't fall asleep like I'd planned,
but when you're all cried out,
you start to *Ooooo*, move tones
from diaphragm, chest, mouth; you discover

this air around you, in you and you
practise your volume a different way
and I think, *That's right my lovely, sing,*
be enough for yourself.

Sasha Dugdale

LIFTING THE BEDCOVERS AND THERE

Lifting the bedcovers and there
The scent of little bodies, their secretions
Their feet, bellies, mouths and hair
Animals overwintering for the season
Of a single night, and how the air
Surges into, under, like water through the horses
Of Augeas, cold on the sweet, fetid, bare
Skins, and that smell is fled contorted
With a small grimace out to the spare
Grey morning, all I embrace
Evaporating in the cool earth's care
Less animal now the opening faces
Their clothes lie folded on the chair
Not yet awake, nor soon aware.

Agnieszka Studzinska

BOAT

Our son climbs into our bed like an oar that has slipped
from its boat, sometimes, I come to bed & find him
already there – a throwback of his father, asleep
& handsome. On some nights our daughter comes in –
bodies like briar, a river below, & I know that this midnight
rowing won't last – the overture of this love shifted,
like a surge of stars in the river itself, our boat mooring.

Hilary Menos

WHITE PEBBLE

Tonight, after the bath and the bedtime story,
somewhere in the space between hanging
and folding damp towels, I kneel down. From here
it is barely a breath, a tipping forward,
until my forehead rests on the bathroom floor.

In our story the children threw down a trail for themselves,
escaped from the woods and found their way back home.
I fold the corner of the page to mark our place
and gently smooth the hair from a sleeping face.
Nobody knows how a story ends.

Here's a pocketful of pebbles, and here's a mountain of crusts.
Here are small white pills to be taken twice a day.
There's rosemary, that's for remembrance.
I follow your trail to the copse and kneel down
and rest my forehead on a carpet of moss.

The Mud Man whispers to me in a dead language.
Noli timere, he hisses. But I am afraid.
I do not know how I got here and I will not pray.

Jacqueline Saphra

WHAT TIME IS IT IN NOVA SCOTIA?

Here, it's 3am, my love, and I can't stop thinking of walruses: historical accounts of sailors who'd trap a calf and torture it until it screamed; the adult animals who heaved their terrible bulk ashore to save their young.

I won't mention nobody's caught the man you ran from but if you come home I swear I'll keep you safe. But I mustn't say come home. Does the heating work? I won't ask about your cough, whether you're eating oranges and learning French or if you like the vest I sent. I wish I could brush your hair. Remind me to send you recipes for soup.

The adult walrus had no predators but man: so many dead, the hunters couldn't take them all and left them piled and useless on the ecoucherie which is French for shore I think but you know that by now if you're learning French.

I won't ask about the terms of your employment, or if you're really healing, or about the lock on your front door and your broken heart, not saying you have a broken heart but if you ever do, that's a lovely, normal thing.

I must go back to sleep, not think about your bicycle, broken locks, dark nights, intruders, walruses. Were they parents too, I wonder, the men who sailed their galleons home laden with carcasses: meat for the voyage, skins for leather, ivory to decorate the wrists of ladies, oil to light the lamps of Europe,

where I am now, oceans away from you at this quiet hour, heavy with the weight of walruses, aching to lay them down, knowing such burdens are not so easily offloaded, the hold of any beast or child, the helpless love one creature must bear another.

Sinéad Morrissey

THE CAMERA

Daughter, for the trick of making me travel
in three directions at once, I raise my glass.
While you were singing Jesus Loves Us

in Miss Hasson's P1 class, I unearthed
from your wardrobe, like a water jar
buried at Thebes, our digital camera,

missing since July and bandaged in socks.
(Arch sequesterer! My 1940s watch
and every figurine your brother ever loved

have passed the way of this already: wrapped
up in whatever lay to your nimble hand
and 'put to sleep' in corners, under the stairs,

in pots in kitchen cupboards,
as though a bouncy ball or Nintendo stylus
contained the capacity to pronounce your guilt

and swaddling meant silence.)
You'd taken over two hundred shots
at different intervals, and in the quiet

of my childless house I sat with it on my lap
to notice what you'd noticed in my absence.
Like Violet Beauregard being squeezed

to her former size in some basement
of the factory by the Oompa Loompas,
you brought me down: key-holes

and door-handles, the hysterical 'O'
of the washing machine stopped mid-cycle,
sofa arms like ledges around a building,

window sills, their proffered assemblages—
pine cones, driftwood, rocks—
the waist-high were your common subjects

and while I watched, the air above me stretched
and left me stranded in a palace,
in airy rooms designed to make me small,

with space above my head for butlers' breath
and tinkly hammered bells, for chandeliers...
You took me behind the scenes

of the lies this family tells about itself—
that the floors are clean and the windows polished—
by snapping us off-guard. Look,

here's me in my stay-at-home dress
with odd socks on and my hair unwashed,
backgrounded, stacking the dishwasher

in a whirligig of mess, while you've
lined up seven pencils to be photographed.
And even though it's only been six months

since most of these were taken
(and here's your father wearing his resting face,
bejowled and middle-aged, chopping an onion,

not seeing what you're doing,
or what made me laugh the most:
the photos of *your* photos on the sideboard,

your own bright smile framed twice),
you've nevertheless led me back
to an earlier time, before we swapped

the kitchen table for a sturdier one
or painted the doorframes brown,
when you were four, unschooled, unkempt,

absorbing this house and your place
in it; bewitched by the marvellous –
and then stealing it.

Degna Stone

RUBY, AGED 4½

She's a roulette wheel loaded against you
A sure-fire bet when you don't have the stake
A gun in the hands of a man with a grudge
Like a smudge of silver leaf on a blacksmith's neck

She's a giggle that turns into a manic episode
An intermittent broadband connection
A delivery between nine in the morning and six at night
Like a bus driver who waits when he sees you running

She's a garden wall with loose brickwork
A ninety minute wait for a cab on your birthday
A higher than expected energy bill
Like a footballer with a doctorate in theology

She's an argument with your boyfriend's brother
A cobra squatting in a meerkat's den
A hooded teen walking behind you at night
Like a coin without a date stamp

She's a bit of a laugh that ends up in court
A train that blasts past at your station
A flag at full mast when the queen is dead
Like the difference between a common puffball
and a death cap. Like being alive.

Rebecca Stonehill

WRITER AND MOTHER: HOW CHILDREN CAN HELP (AND NOT HINDER) THE CREATIVE PROCESS

The birth of my first child came as somewhat of a shock. I was relatively young (at least, by today's standards) and was of the naïve opinion that a baby in my life wouldn't impact on writing, travelling, hiking, working in the allotment, piano playing or indeed any of these things that I took for granted in my life. After all, babies were portable, right?

It didn't take long for me to come back to earth with a bump and realise that, no matter how much my baby slept and how good natured she was, my life had changed irrevocably and time for myself must be lived out in a drastically altered and reduced framework.

The novel I was writing, which had gathered so much steam in the months preceding my daughter's birth, juddered to a halt as life became a whirlwind of feeding, changing, cleaning and responding to the varied demands of a small baby. Like many new mothers, I was also very sleep-deprived. I found not only was I unable to nap during the day when my baby slept, but I also struggled with dropping off at night, so sensitized was I to my baby's round-the-clock needs, struggling to really relax and therefore enjoy the new experience of motherhood in the way I wanted.

I was also upset to discover that I no longer had the desire or energy to write, something a few months previously would have seemed inconceivable. I railed against this, fighting this lack of creative desire in any way I knew how, using those insomniac hours in the middle of the night to open my laptop only to stare at it in frustration as day broke and I found that what I had produced was forced at best and lacklustre at worst. Everywhere I looked there seemed to be women doing it better than me; balancing children and jobs and homes and relationships with flair and energy and then there was me, with just one child and not managing to even hammer out a few worthwhile lines of prose alongside this.

I desperately wanted to continue with my novel but was stuck in a resentful, exhausted rut. I had always been an avid diary writer, but it was my husband who suggested it: Why not start a blog? I was incredulous. Why would I want to potentially bare my soul to complete strangers, and what would I even find to write about? *Write about your insomnia,* my husband persisted, *write about the things you find difficult about motherhood.* I mulled it over.

Perhaps he was right; after all, motherhood, as I was learning pretty quickly, wasn't all about first smiles and sweet little fingers grasping onto your thumbs.

Tentatively, I began writing my blog which I called *Notes of an insomniac mother* and the relief was instantaneous: a flood of exhaustion and joy and frustration all rolled into one as my thoughts and emotions found refuge on the page. Slowly, I began to hear from other mothers around the world who were also suffering from chronic insomnia and knowing that I wasn't alone proved deeply gratifying in a way that would never have materialised had I continued to write solely for myself.

Not only that, but through my blog I learnt to stop giving myself such a hard time about not continuing with my novel. It wasn't going anywhere; I didn't have a deadline and in fact, this break, I soon learnt, gave my novel necessary composting and breathing space. It also helped me to navigate a path through my extreme exhaustion and accompanying doubts about my abilities as a mother, putting a much-needed perspective on my experiences: that this time would pass.

As my daughter grew and I went on to have two more children, time for writing continued to be limited. But I discovered something interesting. Prior to children, my right-hand companion to my writing process was procrastination. With three small children to care for and a supportive husband who took them out on Saturday mornings so I could write, I didn't have TIME to procrastinate anymore. Here was my precious opportunity and I had to seize it with both hands.

Those mornings came to form a vital pulse of my writing, with many short stories and sections of my novel springing from them. The week was for making notes and thinking, but my writing morning was for knuckling down and getting the words on the page.

Not only that, but I also found that my three children provided the inspiration for many ideas. Thinking about my relationship with them breathed new life into the delicate workings of parent-children relations in my novel and short story ideas formed with children as the protagonists. When my husband's job took us to India for a year, I decided that rather than writing about my own experiences, why not blog from the perspective of my three-year-old daughter as she filtered a myriad of new sights, sounds and smells?

Now living in Nairobi, I am doing the same with my middle child. Not only does this provide an opportunity to empathise with my children as they experience a new country and culture, but it is deeply satisfying to write and is something for my children to keep once I print the blogs into physical books.

Motherhood has, over the years, greatly impacted on my writing. But rather than just throwing up challenges, I have learnt to take these challenges alongside the unexpected opportunities that have ensued. Our children are only young once; let's treasure this time whilst also taking a step back from our writing and asking how our children can help rather than hinder our creative process.

Mist rises, smelling of petrol's
burnt offerings, new born,

oily and huge, the lorries drum
on Stokes' Croft,

out of the bathroom mirror the sky
is blue and pale as a Chinese mountain.

and I breathe in.

It's time to go now. I take nothing
but breath, thinned.
A blown-out dandelion globe
might choose my laundered body to grow in.

Carolyn Jess-Cooke

HARE

I kept you in bed with me so many nights,
certain I could hold the life into you,
certain that the life in you wanted to leap out, hare-like,
go bobbing off into some night-field.
For want of more eyes, more arms
I strapped you to me while I did the dishes, cooked, typed,
your little legs frogging
against the deflating dune of your first home.
Nested you in a car seat while I showered, dressed,
and when you breastfed for hours and hours
I learned how to manoeuvre the cup and book around you.
Time and friends and attitudes, too.
We moved breakables a height, no glass tables.
Fitted locks to the kitchen cupboards, door jammers,
argued about screws and pills someone left within reach.
I'll not tell you how my breath left me, how my heart stopped
at your stillness in the cot, and who I became
when at last you moved. There is no telling
what skins of me have dropped and shed in the fears
I've entered. What I will say is that the day
beyond these blankets, beyond our door
is known to me now, fragile as moth-scurf,
its long ears twitching, alert,
white tail winking across the night-field.

Rosie Sandler

MATERNAL INSTINCTS

Having children turns you mad.
Nobody warns you.

It isn't the fear of losing them
– a child-snatcher or a speeding car –

but of losing yourself somewhere:
squeezed into a narrow space;

leaning from a high ledge;
reaching for another pill;

or simply out there, in the open
– where the world is newly unplotted

and all roads lead through fog.

Deryn Rees-Jones

AFTERTHOUGHT

for my daughter

I am following with my finger the blue veins
that travel from wrist to stoop of palm
as you lie now, little milk-drunk carcass,
in an accident of sleep. This is what mothers do

or what I've learned to do, to search your body
for signs of life, wary of pulse and breath
as all the time you follow me,
your mouth, insistent, through the night.

See! I have pressed the soft vowels of your imagination
and made them part of me. They pull me open, stitch me up,
your animal grunts and hungry gestures –
so much a noise that might come from my own mouth,

I can't tell us apart. When I do, daughter, I'll admit, I'm lost,
my new body wandering the forest,
dropping trails of bright stones
till I find you again, a new friend in an old place.

And for how many nights will it be this way,
this slow process of making and undoing,
the soft osmosis of your fragile body? My willing you not
to slip away, turning my own blue veins

to ice? I watch sand gather at your eyes' corners,
shadows making your face from nothing,
those eyes, which might turn any colour,
flickering, half-open, in the pages of your sleep.

I let them rise inside me, birds cased in glass.
And all the while snow falls, depositing on lawns and roofs
its subtle metamorphic chemistry.
Days drift to your smiles.

And I watch the pink coil of your ear,
the snub nose of beginnings;
count to myself in this lonely country
the hoots of an owl, a line of trees,

the bright rings of your growth.

Rachel Zucker

THE DAY I LOST MY DÉJÀ VU

The box is like this today.
The box I live in.
Today: like this.

And though similar, so achingly alike,
ad infinitum, line over the nine, *again*,
it's always
nothing like
before,

nothing, not even the surprise
of another, so similar day of box-living.

Once, I was marked
and markedly different
and at times
while hopscotching
the grouted mosaic
felt *my god* I've seen
before a pattern
just like this

       I've been here!

But no more.

       now, I have never been anywhere
    else. ever but here and though I carry on
      can't return.

  even the day my firstborn son broke me
opened and split shocked shattered that quaint notion of 'before'
     is no more than a rung of how I got
  a mother's now-mind, a strung-together-bead's walk.

      this moment. this. this. this.
                is not what I
              expected…

today my beautiful child eviscerates me.

a charmer, a snake, he fits my living heart
into his fist blunt fangs and I go willingly
into love with him. he is
every day a new child
and every day I'm still in love means
nothing like before.

remember when we
used to

remember
things, every night, say
remember the time...
and the smells of the past and sometimes a portal
opened up

and we slipped in there, into the past
rose up to meet us we were not
so all alone then, our lives had meaning
and we were not born again every goddamn
day but felt it what it was like to be there
in those lost places, the gone?

remember? those days? but I can't.

now all of me but this is gone and I was never a girl.

never but mother never

every same day new again. every way is without a way out or
way to look back, to *be* back, to bring the fabric into a tight
pucker or pocket or foxhole or hem, some little space to fall into a breath
like an open grave or little death. instead I learn bird names
for the shapes and colors and songs around me though every bird
is different from every bird. I learn the map. watch the armies advance,

forward! they bellow and jab mercilessly with their spear points,
go on!

carry! and so it is I haul my sons step after day each day so swept away by love
and terror I would sometimes rather kill us all then go on like this
marching, marching, new, new, new, day, and when they
are just too heavy to carry I become stronger
than is possible and carry on

LOSS, ABSENCE, SUFFERING

Pippa Little

FOR MY MISCARRIAGE

you-dot in yolk

dark snag in the flare nebula

my body the light bulb

that burned you up

my want the dark matter crowding

your feeble constellation

so one by one each cell fizzled out

we crashed in bloody sea-swell

I surfaced without you

Nuala Ellwood

THE WEIGHT OF A GIRL

Babies are supposed to be warm, I told them, as they placed you on my stomach. They are supposed to cry out and suckle and look up with milky-blue eyes. But you, the girl who had hidden in my womb for seven months, didn't stir though you were fully formed. She is just sleeping, I told myself, as they wrapped you in a hospital-issue blanket and took you away. And I almost believed the lie.

The midwife told me that some women can't carry female babies; that their bodies can't sustain them and I carried that thought with me and made myself the guilty party. My body was a toxic place, a frozen wilderness where children shrivelled and died and so I would no longer nourish it; I would punish the body that had failed my child.

Hungry and exhausted I longed for the release of sleep when you would return to me in my dreams. Sometimes you were alive and thriving; other times you just lay there like you did that first day. And I wished for you to come back. I saw you on tube trains, on buses and in parks: a little girl with black curls and a radiant smile. One day I watched from Albert Bridge as a beautiful doomed whale thrashed and blustered in the alien waters of the Thames and its stillness in death reminded me of you.

And then one scorching May morning you came back to me. I saw you standing in the corner of a bright delivery room as my healthy baby boy took his first gasp. Your eyes burned into my soul as he flopped heavily onto my chest and his heat seared my skin. I felt your resentment as I put him to my breast and filled him with the goodness I couldn't give to you. You were with me as I waited for them to examine him and we held our breath until they told us all was fine.

But the whisper of you echoed through the halls of his early years; an incomplete picture that I needed to fill. And though we left it to chance I knew as I held the test in my hands and looked at the faint blue cross that the baby growing inside me was another you. I couldn't tell anyone the news, even at three months, as an unquiet voice gnawed at my temples telling me that this would never be.

Some people are not built to carry girls, another nurse told me, as summer breathed its last and my boy child played hopscotch in a hospital garden. And I believed her as I lay on a sterile bed looking at a screen where a child hung suspended in amniotic fluid.

'Babies are like parasites,' said an overworked GP, three days earlier, as he offered me indigestion tablets to make me go away. 'They can survive on very little. Don't worry. This baby is going nowhere.'

But I knew she was leaving me as more blood came away and I saw you in the corner of the bathroom as I crouched on the floor. 'Never,' you whispered, like Poe's raven. 'Never again.' And I listened to you because you were the voice I trusted, above all others.

'You'll be taken down to surgery,' said the doctor, leaving the door open as I undressed so the world could see my failure. 'Then we can scrape the matter away.'

We took our matter and we gave her a name: Nerina. The sea nymph, the girl whose being was too heavy to bear. And we took her down to the river that runs through our city and let the water carry her away. She is there as you are here in my head, two girls swimming in different directions but never coming home.

Some women aren't meant to carry girls. I heard the well-meaning voices shout in my head as I took my boy's hand and walked back to the house. And as he chatted excitedly about train rides and chocolate cake and an egg with two yokes, the words grew lighter, they twisted and contracted until all that was left, all that existed, was a mother and her child beating back the unbidden explanations with the weight of their love.

Catherine Graham

LULLABY

after Postnatal Depression

You arrived, gifted.
Innocent as time
we waited
for fortune to cradle us together.

Instead
your baby blanket became a pane of glass:

I sang a startled lullaby
as the stars kissed you goodnight.

Lost
in a kind of wilderness
you gently led me home.

How wisely you reminded me
that even sand and water
in time
become solid, unbreakable stone.

Becky Cherriman

THE FOSTER MOTHER'S BLANKET

It is not just a corporeal thing but a thing made of smells:
lentils rubbed in cumin; shagpile and other children's hair.
In its folds, ghosts of rotting lino and pickings from bins,
which have never touched this blanket
but are there anyway, made bearable
by the whispered comfort of her hand cream.

Underneath, the promise of knots sliced
through – a vessel unmoored, its cargo a bundle
to be delivered out of shaking hands;
this blanket – a torn sail
and loss and loss and loss and loss.

Yes, the salt of yesterday will catch
in everyone's throats
til it drifts into something new –
mashed potato and Top Trumps. Home.

Before a child is adopted, the foster parent sleeps with a blanket for several nights. When the child goes to their new home, they take the blanket and are reassured by its familiar smell.

Wendy Pratt

SIXTH BIRTHDAY

You would still be small enough
to pull onto my knee; a kindling
of hot, slim limbs, your shape
not quite removed from babyhood.

I would brush sand from the soles
of your feet, rub the salt
from your shins with a towel, try
to hold on to this seaside-smiles girl.

Maybe ice cream; a hot fudge sundae
at the *Harbour Bar*. Your heart-shaped face,
and mine, reflected in the mirrors there,
your dad, distracted by the football

on his phone. He kisses you to grins,
we pack our ordinary life into
our ordinary car, drive home
to arguments about bedtime,

a hot bath, light sleeping,
a *Beatrix Potter* bedroom,
drawers full of clothes

that you still might wear.

Kaddy Benyon

STRANGE FRUIT

Sometimes I have an urge to slip
my hands inside the soiled, wilting
necks of your gardening gloves; to
let my fingers fill each dusty burrow,
then close my eyes and feel
a blush of nurture upon my skin.

Sometimes I am so afraid my envy
will hack at your figs, strawberries,
or full-bellied beans, I dig my fists
in my pockets and nip myself. Sometimes
I imagine the man who belongs to
the hat hanging on the bright-angled

nail in your shed. I think about you
toiling and sweating with him;
coaxing growth from warm earth;
pushing life into furrows. I am curious
about what cultivates and blooms
there in your enclosed, raised bed –

yet I want no tithe of it for myself.
Sometimes I just want to show
you the places I'm mottled, rotten
and bruised; I want you to lean close
enough to hold the strange fruit
of me and tell me I may yet thrive.

Geraldine Clarkson

MONICA'S OVERCOAT OF FLESH

Am I still a mother if the girl I reared happened
to sicken and die, fast-tracking there as she did
everything else? There is no word for it,
not widowed, nor barren, nor maid, no moniker
to give a warning to would-be interlocutors.
Bond of selkie-silk, little twin with double
helping of brass. Could she, *cushla*,
have inveigled the boatman, like she would,
slipped a nod, a wink, a broken-stem dandelion;
rusticate, tangle-haired, red-cheeked, tearing
out of childhood, eschewing what wilts.
Shrugging off the fussy overcoat.
Monica. For the last time, will you
come when I call you. Bold child.

Elizabeth Barrett

GOOD THINGS HAPPENED ON THAT DAY ALSO

Through a crowded carriage window
as it pulled away, a glimpse
of my daughter. Later that day
a drizzle of sun like ginger honey
on the Dales. From a distant train
a trail of steam hemming a seam of sky.
The village shop where I bought
curd tart and apricots.
A woman bleeding at the leg
picking nettles with her bare hands
from the ground: the way I felt
my stalled heart jumpstart itself.

And then, as I crossed Ivelet Bridge,
the heron which stopped to watch.
At a bend in the road, a hedgerow of stars
opening like white flowers.
Light rain like scattered moonstone
across a wooded scar. That afternoon,
the birds which came suddenly
to my window, scrabbling against the glass.
How I worked my cross-stitch strand
by strand until I slept, needle in hand.
That I dreamed her face not knowing,
then, the glimpse had been my last.

Carrie Etter

A BIRTHMOTHER'S CATECHISM

How did you let him go?

With black ink and legalese

How did you let him go?

It'd be another year before I could vote

How did you let him go?

With altruism, tears and self-loathing

How did you let him go?

A nurse brought pills for drying up breast milk

How did you let him go?

Who hangs a birdhouse from a sapling?

Melissa Lee-Houghton

ACCIDENT

You wet the bed this morning and I only found out
this afternoon, picking up your pyjamas from the carpet,
smelling the chlorine caught in the fabric, held there
for me to find. To know.

When I kiss you on your hair you smell like nothing else I know.
I have never written a poem about you
because you're innocent. And my poems aren't innocent.
This morning when I woke

you were lying in my bed next to me—
the morning a rainbow on the ceiling;
it felt like the beginning of summer, and the air
through the window was clear as

the thoughts of someone considering suicide.
Baby if I don't wake up
in the morning someday don't read any of my poems.
Don't remember that I was always tired,

would put a film on the DVD player
to keep you occupied while I slept,
waking as tired as ever and as sad as your face this morning
when you hadn't plucked up the courage to tell me

you'd wet the bed.

Marie Naughton

STILL

On the third day I woke to his weary face,
watching from an armchair by the hospital bed.

You know how dreams have boldness
that melts to uncertainty, the minute you speak?

I blurted my epiphany – *we've fallen
through a gap in the language* – like that

was that. Orphan, widow, widower. No word
for parent whose child has died. The midwife

wheeled her to me for the final time.
I didn't want to notice

her mouth had opened slightly, the darkness
of the silent space

behind her perfect lips.
On the ninth day, after the cremation,

my mother-in-law announced they slipped
her stillborn daughter in a stranger's coffin.

Standard practice in the Sixties. After the ninth day
days rolled together like blobs of Play-Doh.

The clinic sent an invitation for a check-up.
A receptionist phoned with a reminder –

and don't forget to bring the baby.
Passers-by burbled with our toddler in shops,

on buses. She parroted the sentence – *my mummy
had a baby in her tummy but it flew to heaven.*

Eyes would dart across at me, she'd stick
her bottom lip out, rub a fist against her cheek.

At twenty-nine, pregnant with her second child,
she'll totter on the edge of a memory, when it blows up

like a draught of stale air from a lift shaft.
No word for sister left behind.

Anger was my comfort, I couldn't help
but swaddle it round me. I shook off

the group that met each week for coffee
as our bellies swelled. One woman dropped by

with a card. I watched her stutter the buggy
up our narrow path. I ran the shower

as she pressed the bell. They clubbed together
and Interflora delivered lilies. I ripped them to bits,

rammed the shredded stalks and petals in the bin.
– *Fan out your fingers, float on each pain* –

the midwife instructed when I was in labour.
At Waterstones I ransacked the shelves,

poetry, pop psychology. I delved for answers,
not images, no empty creels, no seed-flesh,

no bone-curd, words were vacant shells.
– *Chill, stupor, letting go* – Dickinson

came close, but not till later.
For eighteen months I kept no journal,

started taking risks. Wantonly
I walked under ladders, gave up greeting magpies.

In Barcelona our teacher told us if we dreamt
in Spanish, we'd arrived. All my dreams

were black and white. Black and white.
Afternoons watching classics: Random Harvest,

Mr Chips, Brief Encounter. Celia Johnson
as Laura, mending linen by the fire.

Fred with a crossword in his armchair
after her affair – can you call it that? –

is over. I drowned in that concerto, played,
replayed those final scenes – *There'll come a time*

in the future when I shan't mind about this anymore

Karen McCarthy Woolf
MOTHERS' DAY

Mother's Day was always a bit of a fluster when I was growing up. Not because my mum demanded roses and breakfast in bed – she was always too much of a rebel/hippy/feminist for that – but because it was always touch and go as to whether my grandma's cards would arrive before Sunday. I say 'cards' because Nan also liked to get one from us, preferably saying 'to the world's best Nan on Mother's Day'. Our inevitably late, hand-drawn affairs, or tasteful art cards 'blank inside', were a poor cousin to the pre-written poetry embossed in gold that arrived on the Thursday from my aunty. Now, since my grandma passed away age 91, Mum is surprisingly keen for us to mark the occasion, and I pause, wistfully, at the 'grandmother's-day' cards in Smith's.

I never dreamed that I might not be a mother and in fact what I really aspired to was becoming a grandmother. I would be the wise matriarch presiding over generations of chicks. When I lost my only son Otto in a full-term stillbirth in 2009, everything I'd taken for granted about motherhood up to that point evaporated. This sense of maternal loss was compounded by the fact that my mother-in-law died from a sudden and voracious brain tumour when I was six months pregnant. Almost overnight the illusion that having and becoming a mother were things we could take for granted lay by the wayside.

An Aviary of Small Birds is the book I wrote in response to these life-changing events, and particularly the loss of my son. It was a way for me to process the experience and because the stillbirth occurred at a crucial time in my career, where I was focusing on a first collection, it also prompted a new poetic. Whereas previously I had sometimes used form as a foil to avoid facing uncomfortable emotions, it was now a tool I could employ to help access and transform the most profound pain. And as I see it, if the work is to transcend catharsis and become art, then that transformation must take place. Equally, if it is to be poetry then what is felt (not just what is thought) needs to be tangible.

Writing *Aviary* also inspired a new understanding of family and what it means to be a mother. At the time I was part of the Complete Works mentoring programme that exists to widen cultural diversity in poetry publishing. I will always be grateful for the sense of extended familial support that came from being part of that community.

In the book itself, the natural world is a persistent backdrop to many of the poems. I realise now that that connection with birds, trees, the sea, rivers, the moon was a way of me holding on to what remained certain at a time when that which was human was anything but secure. Working in my garden, nurturing plants and flowers, was also a way for me to express a maternal instinct.

Currently I'm researching new ways of writing about nature in the face of climate change. *An Aviary of Small Birds* is a book that seeks to make sense of a very intimate loss and make the experience of grief universally accessible to others; my new work seeks to process a very universal loss – ecological devastation on a global scale – and somehow render it personal. If we are to survive as a species then we need to extend the care we offer to our own offspring to a wider community that includes all the life forms on Earth, so many of which are now perilously under threat. That, for me, is being a mother.

Karen McCarthy Woolf

WHITE BUTTERFLIES

Three white butterflies
flutter then land
on the artichoke spikes
in the walled garden.

White sky against the ash.
The wind in the leaves
a rush of sighs.

White lavender
at the edge of the pool.
White hydrangeas
wilted in the bouquet.
White lilies sticky with scent.
White tissues in the box.
White linen on the bed.
White curtains shrunk in the wash.
White muslin squares.
Your tiny white vests, unworn.

Jane Burn

ONLY CHILD

I listen to you singing to yourself. Watch you in the garden, finding
a teammate in the fence as it returns the ball to you – standing in for
the brother or sister I never gave you. Couldn't give you.

Something broke after you. I tell you how I could never have made
something so magical twice, that you grew so tall and strong
because you are all my babies born at once.

Julia Darling

ADVICE FOR MY DAUGHTERS

Don't believe the first things,
don't believe the last things,
believe what you see.

Don't sit too close to drains
or spend too long at a stove.
Always know where the exit is.

Don't store too much.
Know what to give away.
Hold as much as you can carry.

If you have children give them magic,
soft songs, a coin under a pillow,
but don't give them everything.

Sleep in good linen, enjoy the smell of lemon,
breathe deeply, dream deeply,
if you don't know what to do, do something.

Don't diet, or be a martyr.
Life is suffering, but you are lucky
so you might as well be happy.

MOTHER'S WORK

Anna Barker

THE 'WRITER ME' AND THE 'MOTHER ME'

I have actually resented being a mother. There, I said it. That sounds awful and ungrateful, but I felt being a mother stopped me from being a writer. I'd sit watching *Fireman Sam* and somehow feel I was being restrained from getting inside my own thoughts long enough to be creative. Sure, I could be creative with toilet rolls and an empty yoghurt pot, but that wasn't who I really was.

Except it wasn't that simple. The 'who I was' had already long gone.

Shortly after the publication of my second novel, *Before I Knew Him*, my life had exploded. In fact, if my life had been a novel I doubt it would have done very well. It was simply too dramatic, too unbelievable – even for fiction. Three weeks after my daughter, Jessie, was born (wonderful but ever so slightly upheaving), my father died. I became a parent and lost a parent and I had absolutely no idea how to reconcile the two. After the funeral, to which Jessie had accompanied me, wrapped in a white blanket, there was the small matter of grief. I would stare at her gurgling in the Moses basket for hours on end until, eventually, sobbing, I'd be convinced I saw my father's eyes staring back.

When she was 10 months old Jessie's father moved on. Alone and still inside the first year of grief and motherhood, I fumbled around for a way forward. Over the next few years I tried to resurrect the writer in me, but it was no good. Two novels stalled at 20,000 words (no shortage of paper for Jessie to scribble on the back of). I'd lost my voice. I wrote wooden prose or I tried overly hard to write what I felt. My senses were all dulled, I saw beauty in nothing, I could not empathise with the world around me, I had no patience for inventing characters. So I did what anyone does when they're just say getting by: I focussed on the one thing that seemed to matter more than anything else – the happiness of my daughter – and writing faded into the background.

So the truth is that I still don't know whether it was the grief that squashed my creative self, or becoming a mother, but it had gone and as Jessie began to walk and talk it became even more difficult to resurrect it. She was all-consuming. I could not turn my attention from her for a second; she had me on a short rope as all toddlers do, but the result was there was no room inside my head to think. I couldn't connect thoughts together reliably, never mind create an 80,000-word story. The 'mother me' and the 'writing me' (if she still existed) were entirely different people. I was either one or the other, but I could never be both.

But then something rather random and wonderful happened. I'd gone to London on a course and had been required to take my novels with me. On the way home on the train I found myself bored with nothing to read but my own book – *Before I Knew Him*. I started reading. I saw the writer I had been, I heard my voice again. I also saw how much of my writing was immersed in the natural world. That's who I was.

I'm now writing a novel I believe in and instead of viewing the countless hours I've spent roaming woods with Jessie as wasted writing time (though terrific mother time) I can see now how I can merge the two. I've even started writing a blog called *Wild Child*, which is about how to strengthen the connection children have with the natural world. The fodder for the blog comes from the adventures I take with Jessie. Crucially, these adventures are bringing those dulled senses to life again and enabling me to play to my strengths as a writer.

I've also changed my writing habits. No, sorry, I should say I have learned to write under entirely new conditions. I do not wait for the muse to arrive, I write. I do not make endless notes and keep journals, I write. I do not sit down at my computer and decide to come back to it later when I have more time because I won't have more time, so I write.

Now Jessie is learning to write and together we keep a 'Happy Book' in which we write down the things that make us happy. We'll be reading them to each other on Christmas Day this year. In these small ways, the blog and the Happy Book, I'm making writing part of *both* of our lives.

Marianne Burton

MEDITATION ON THE HOURS
5PM: THE LIE OF THE POOL

I have been disillusioned since the age of ten.
My mother was an artist. She saw things differently.
When I came in from swimming she would often
ask what the water looked like, was the sea
angry or pleased? I always turned away.
I never could be bothered to humour her.
It was the school pool, mother, I would say,a
ugly, noisy, with heel plasters in the water.

But she, rinsing out my costume,
saw the barnacled undersides of whales,
quickslip of dolphins, flumes
of canoes, hammocking sails,
and she would paint them for me
on her canvases, in thick oils, badly.

Hollie McNish

31 MAY

Stand back. Back off. Breathe out –
You're almost out the door now.
Be there. to help. if asked –
She's only two years old now.
She wants. to try. herself –
So let your arms drop down now.
Stand back. Back off. Breathe out –
There's no point getting stressed now.
She's almost. done. her buttons –
It doesn't matter some are wrong now.
If you. hurry her. she'll panic –
Her shoes are almost on now.
The left. is on. the right –
But no need to step in yet.
She's already looking down now –
Now she's. trying out. the left.
Don't let. your blood. get hot.
Don't let. your patience. blow.
Relax. Breathe out. Be proud.
She's only two years old.

Last week, I had to fight a very strong urge to ditch work, go to the pub and scream into a pint for three hours. Sometimes getting a toddler ready is like that. Sometimes it is totally fine. Sometimes it is an utter joy to watch little fingers scrabble to button jackets wonkily and push shoes on the wrong feet and then stand up, proud as peacock, to display their talent. Sometimes it is hard not to move their fingers aside and do it much more quickly for them. Let her do it, Dee will remind me. Let her do it, I'll remind him. Teamwork.

Little One wants to do everything herself now. It is a beautiful thing. But everything takes a tad longer because of that. It is hard to be patient sometimes. I want her to learn life skills – dressing herself, tying her shoes, getting her bag ready – I really do. But Lord God, sometimes it takes so long to get ready! Sometimes it takes gritted teeth, deep breaths and the constant thought that it is OK to be late, she is learning, she is learning. Resist. the. urge. to. help. her.

People often say that parents or carers who 'leave employment' in order to raise their kids are losing valuable skills and CV points and job training.

Personally, the task of managing to get my toddler ready as she breaks down in tears (because she could not work out which way her pants go on), goes into a strop (because I tried to help), slams her door, hides in her bed in protest, then takes an hour to brush her teeth, and out of the door without losing my temper, raising my hand, crying hysterically or throwing myself on the kitchen floor – is a miracle. And we were still only a bit late in dropping her off at Grandma's. To me, that's a skill and should definitely be seen credibly on a CV.

I think that after that morning I finally felt ready to apply for the job of chief ambassador of the UN peacekeeping conflict resolution force. As stated in Article 1 of the UN Charter, the UN is expected 'to maintain international peace and security... to take effective collective measures for the prevention and removal of threats to peace... and to bring about by peaceful means... adjustment or settlement of international disputes.'

Now, I went to what I think is a good school – St Bart's Comprehensive, Newbury. I worked geekily hard and with a lot of help from family and teachers and the fact that I had my own bedroom to work in, got into Cambridge University to study languages. After I graduated, I then worked in a nightclub and a shop to pay for a part-time MSc in Development Studies with Economics at the School of Oriental and African Studies in London. I read lots of papers and studies about international conflict. I wanted to work in that area somehow.

None of those qualifications – plus the fact that I could not afford to do a free internship with any charity after graduating – made me feel capable of applying for the kind of the job I wanted. I was always sure I wasn't good enough, no matter how hard I worked. My supervisor at Cambridge used to call it the 'state-school mentality'. But doing the morning drop-off day after day without losing my temper, I finally feel ready. In fact, I feel that the new skills I have now acquired as a parent should be a mandatory part of any application for a UN or government position requiring any sort of negotiation or discussion skills. Instead of unaffordable internship placements for extremely well-off graduates (no grudge here), I now imagine an interview might go something a bit more like this:

Hello, please come in. Which position are you applying for?
Er, Head of the UN peacekeeping mission.
And why do you feel qualified for this job?

Well, I graduated from Eton and have a first-class degree in politics from Oxford University, a PhD in conflict resolution and international peacekeeping and I have been on an unpaid internship for an international charity for the last three years, as well as having experience in my father's department of the World Bank from the age of three.

OK, fine. Are you a parent or guardian of a child?

Erm, no. I don't have kids.

Have you ever spent at least three full days and nights as the sole carer of a child or other person in need?

Er, what? No.

Have you ever had a baby's poo spurt up your arms while changing a nappy and still carried on saying 'Googoo' and smiling as they wee in your face?

Er, no.

Have you ever had to get a child dressed and out of the house, been able to keep your cool and react calmly and peaceably under the intense pressure of tantrums and crying and screams and then stand on the pavement as other people walk past you, smiling at them red-faced whilst your child lies on the floor screaming 'Go away, I'm never speaking to you again!' and refuses to move – without crying or screaming yourself?

Er, no.

Have you ever had to settle a dispute with a child or group of children without resorting to fist-banging, shouting 'Ra ra, Mr Speaker', raising your voice or laughing in a pompous, arrogant manner at them?

Er, no.

OK, thank you. We'll let you know. We were really looking for someone who has toddler-care skills. Primary teaching might work too. We'll call you.

Rose Cook

POEM FOR SOMEONE WHO IS JUGGLING HER LIFE

This is a poem for someone
who is juggling her life.

Be still sometimes.
Be still sometimes.

It needs repeating
over and over

to catch her attention
over and over

because someone juggling her life
finds it difficult to hear.

Be still sometimes.
Be still sometimes.

Let it all fall sometimes.

Ruth Stacey

ON THE CAUTIOUS ROAD

The hitchhiker holds his sign hopefully.
It is such a sad little sign;
limp, with a spelling mistake.
Yet it is the way I am going.
If this was 1943 I would stop.
If I was a man I would stop.
Why is he standing there? they ask.
I answer. My children look at me and say
Well, we could give him a lift?
I can't admit that I imagine the worst
that could happen, the things
they don't know about yet;
rare and unlikely but possible
chance of him snuffing out our lights,
their miniature bones lost in the earth.

So I reply that this car is too
noisy for that traveller,
he looks like he has a headache.

We drive straight past.
The children wave.

C.L. Taylor
MOTHERHOOD TURNED ME TO CRIME

Making the leap from romantic comedies to psychological thrillers might not seem like the most logical progression for an author but I was feeling far from logical when I made the decision. My son was four months old and I was severely sleep deprived because he was waking me every two to three hours at night for a feed and had done since birth. I was also the loneliest I'd ever felt in my life.

Life was very different when I started writing romantic comedies. I lived in Brighton and was single and free of responsibility. I had a well-paid job, a close group of friends and my main obsession was finding Mr Right. Writing romantic comedies came naturally. I was terrible at dating, naturally clumsy and highly skilled at saying the wrong thing at the most inopportune moment.

Fast forward several years to 2012 and my life couldn't have been more different. I was living in Bristol with a loving partner and our new baby. We'd moved to Bristol for my partner's job when I was seven months pregnant and I'd left behind my close-knit group of friends and independent life in Brighton. When our son was born I was happier than I'd ever been in my life but the transition to motherhood came as a shock. Suddenly I couldn't leave the house for more than two hours because I was exclusively breastfeeding (my son refused to take a bottle so my partner couldn't help) and, with no close friends nearby, I had to rely on once weekly meetings with my NCT group for a social life. They were lovely ladies but they didn't seem to be struggling as much as me and I didn't want to be the moaning minny who brought the group down. I tried going to local playgroups and classes but swapping a few words with fellow mums wasn't the same as confiding in close friends. And that's when I started writing again.

I took all my new emotions – feelings of guilt, worry, fear, protective-ness and maternal love – and I poured them into the character of Susan. As I sat in the dark, night after night, and fed my son I began plotting *The Accident* (Avon, 2014) in my head. Susan was in danger, so was her daughter and I needed to tell their story. It became so real, so vivid, that I would rush to my laptop during my son's daytime nap and type until his plaintive cry called me back into the real world.

Five months later I typed 'The End' and sent the novel to my agent. I was scared. What if she hated it? What if she told me I'd ruined my career by deciding to switch genres? For two days I worried and waited, pressing 'refresh' on my email inbox more times than was healthy and then there it was, her verdict – 'the best book you've written'. I'd done a lot of crying since my son was born but the tears that fell then weren't because I felt exhausted, isolated or scared.

They were tears of relief.

Janette Ayachi

PLASTICINE LOVE HEARTS

You curved into me like a child
that has never learnt to walk,
a scuttle into my chest
as I folded over you
like a Russian doll.
The first day
I left you there
I came back
to find you crying
nestled on the nursery
teacher's lap like a newborn
regressing, an upside down egg chart.

You were late for their world
as I practised detachment
from tiny chairs and tiny
children asked me
to zip-up jackets
tie laces, tell stories
whilst you learnt
the letters in your name
made plasticine love-hearts
became the keeper of the chicken coup
sifting your fur-less hands over its feathers
feeding it corn and water with curious precision.

Today I am not there
watching you and the time
ticks slowly, my heart now scuttles
in my chest as I align trust and bravery
from its layers like a Russian doll internally displaced
into individual shapes, regiment in its own body-hollow echo
waiting for the bell to siren its puzzle-march to complete single form.
We step back into each other the same way people jump
onto moving trains, a leap toward shelter,
your nails darkened by the hearts
you carved and cloned for me in my absence.

Carrie Fountain
WORKING MOTHER POEM

All I want to do is go home
and take off these pants
and make Tuscan bean soup,
carefully following the recipe
stained darkly with soups
of the past, dicing celery
with the news on while the baby
sits balanced on her
outrageous thighs and plays
Making Tuscan Bean Soup,
which involves pouring all
the tea bags out of their boxes
and into the giant pot I will
eventually have to squat down
and take away from her.
When I do, she will cry,
and her crying face will be
a house with its garage door
rolling open at four a.m.,
flooding the dark street
with fluorescent light.
When I apologize to my daughter
it won't be like the apologies
of my past.

Lily Dunn

THE MUTABLE BED

First a book, then a baby

My school friends called me a writer. How could they not, when I spent most of my childhood and adolescence with a notebook and pen, disappearing into the library, then reading the latest instalments to a crowd in the corridor. In my late twenties, I set myself two goals: write a novel and have a child. My friend Emily, already a mother of two, advised me to do it in that order. I am forever grateful. During my pregnancy, I wished for two things: a healthy baby and a publisher, as if the attainment of both would be a kind of completion. I was gifted with both these things, unaware that the real challenges had only just begun.

The mutable bed

I've always loved a good bed. As a teenager, I claimed my mum and dad's seven-foot mattress, too big for my bedroom, its sides spilling over my queen-sized bed frame. I spent many hours in that bed, smoking, reading, eating oranges. I had my first sexual encounters (when my mum was out), cried myself to sleep from my first broken heart. When I met the man who was to become my husband, I was struck by the emptiness of his bedroom, the neatness of his huge white bed. I soon moved into his room and bed, and messed up the covers, stuck wallpaper to the walls, littered the floor with half-read books and abandoned clothes. We got to know each other in his bed, through long mornings after late nights, reading the paper and dozing back to sleep. Then we had our first baby. After two days of labouring at home, I was overcome with exhaustion and fear, and I saw our bed differently. It hovered there in the gloom, still at the room's centre, but no longer tempting in my pain, no longer a place of comfort. I mourned the place in which I had taken these things for granted. The next day I became a mother; our newborn daughter slept between us on a sheepskin.

A Room of One's Own

It took a while to reclaim our bed: a good four years before we had uninterrupted sleep. I tried, too soon, perhaps, to carve out a place for myself:

a study and a door that remained closed, a Saturday escape to the British Library. For a time my creativity was still locked into my children. But after a few years of frustrated scribbling of notes that only seemed to skirt the surface, my words and characters began to sing again. My voice returned, but it was different, more mature perhaps, a little louder and more credible. I became less precious about how and when I could write and learned to grab the moment, recognising that my dreams had value, that there were many empty hours to mothering that were made more colourful by my growing internal world: when I was pushing a buggy, cooking the kid's dinner, tidying.

Heart to heart

I have loved a million times over, too many boyfriends to count, too many friends. But to love someone more than you love yourself? It opens your eyes to life, to people. With more empathy comes better understanding of our differences, of the hopes and fears behind those everyday faces. With empathy comes honesty and bravery: honesty to open your heart and let it bleed onto the page; bravery to immortalize it into print, to read it to others. My children have slowed me down, chilled me out, and added structure to my life. My writing fits into that structure. And above all else, my children are my muse. To engage with the kind of love and tenderness you feel for your child is to engage with being alive. These are the stories of the heart that stand the test of time, with an honesty that readers recognise.

Tess Gallagher

I STOP WRITING THE POEM

to fold the clothes. No matter who lives
or who dies, I'm still a woman.
I'll always have plenty to do.
I bring the arms of his shirt
together. Nothing can stop
our tenderness. I'll get back
to the poem. I'll get back to being
a woman. But for now
there's a shirt, a giant shirt
in my hands, and somewhere a small girl
standing next to her mother
watching to see how it's done.

.

Kate Bingham

THE WORLD AT ONE

I lie in bed until *The World at One*,
why should my heart go off with an alarm?
The body's woman's work is never done,

the blood gets up to exercise the lungs.
The kettle sings, I count my lucky charms –
a chain connects and separates each one

and when I shake my wrist it shakes the sun
that scatters off the wall and scalds my arm.
It's only skin and coffee, no harm done.

War continues, voting has begun;
my left-hand thumb elects my right-hand palm.
We couldn't all go on to be someone.

I have a little silver house to run,
a silver Scottie dog to keep me calm.
I don't remember everything I've done

but bring me pencil, paper, chewing gum
and I will stay at home and do no harm,
imagining myself a world for one
where what I did was what I should have done.

Sujata Bhatt

29 APRIL 1989

She's three months old now,
asleep at last for the afternoon.
I've got some time to myself again
but I don't know what to do.
Outside everything is greyish green and soggy
with endless Bremen-Spring drizzle.
I make a large pot of Assam tea
and search through the books
in my room, shift through my papers.
I'm not looking for anything, really,
just touching favourite books.
I don't even know what I'm thinking,
but there's a rich round fullness
in the air
like living inside Beethoven's piano
on a day when he was
particularly energetic.

Mary Austin Speaker

AFTER THE FIRST CHILD, THE SECOND

for Chris Martin

To you
through whom

these sudden days
blowse & hum

thirst & quench
a tide of tensing trees

days tick by
beats in a song

my body grows
fuller each day

I think my life
has always been

for this quiet
darkness

your forehead
& eyelashes

face pressed
to my breast

your skin a texture
electrifying

my fingertips
wool on cotton

wool on glass
the fibers rise

& I can't sleep
for being alive

Zoë Brigley

MOTHERHOOD *IS* VALUABLE FOR THE CREATIVE LIFE

Whatever way you look at it, motherhood entails sacrifice. While the all-sacrificing mother is a reductive and unhelpful stereotype, it is a fact that as a mother you have to give up time, space, and energy for your children. This could mean stopping what you are doing every few hours to breastfeed. It could mean being interrupted by a steaming diaper. Or it could be the funneling of creative energy into fort-building, cookie baking, imagining games, and planning adventures. Having two children under five, I know all about this.

In her long poem about domesticity and womanhood, 'Letter from a Far Country,' Gillian Clarke imagines male critics as seagulls that disturb domestic tranquility with their shrieks. 'Where', they call, 'are your great works?', and their cries are 'as cruel as greedy babies'. Clarke questions the compatibility of the writing life with motherhood in a similar way to Kim Brooks's recent piece for *The Cut*. 'Surely there was no reason,' Brooks ponders, 'that a person like myself couldn't be a great wife, a great mother, and also the sort of obsessive, depressive, distracted writer whose persona I'd always romanticized.'

Of course, I sympathize with Brooks. I know how demanding it can be to balance life, work, and children. When she lists the parts of motherhood that she wants to jettison – playdates, birthday parties, parent nights, after-school activities, and worrying about standardized test scores – I am right there with her. But do these ephemeral concerns have to be an inherent part of motherhood? When Brooks rejects the exasperating aspects of parenting, isn't she really describing the demands of bourgeois motherhood, white middle-class motherhood, suburban motherhood?

Does creativity have to be incompatible with domestic life? Once all the consumerist, competitive rubbish is cast off, what might be left behind is a more positive way of parenting that demands focus, mindfulness, and awareness of others. It's a way of life that can be inspiring and empowering, but it entails rejecting stereotypes of creativity that are so often defined in terms of men's lives and experiences.

Brooks is opposed by stereotypes of creativity: Byron, promiscuous and sensational, or Baudelaire walking the streets of Paris. She sees the standard of creativity in Verlaine engaging in stormy affairs, or Faulkner refusing his daughter's demands because 'Nobody remembers Shakespeare's children.' The trouble is that all of these personae entail an individualism that cannot be maintained well in the life of domesticity and being a good parent.

As much as I love Byron and Baudelaire, there is something tiresome and distasteful about romanticizing these men, who in order to define themselves as marked by genius, led lives that were intrinsically selfish. In Brooks' eyes, being a parent and especially a mother means being 'cautious, boring' and 'conventional.' But what if we replaced the word 'cautious' with 'mindful'? The word 'boring' with 'repetitive' or 'cyclic'? The word 'conventional' with 'steady'?

I am not trying to say that combining motherhood and creativity is easy, and in no way do I blame Brooks for the comments she makes. But I do believe that it is possible to make a productive and rich writing life as a mother, and against Brooks' list of women writers troubled by maternity, I would list Toni Morrison, Jhumpa Lahiri, Marilynne Robinson, and Zadie Smith. The point is that we have to try to change expectations: first we must challenge ideas about what mothers do, but we also have to defy stereotypical imaginings of what creativity looks like. The tortured male genius with the sensational life is a dead end as a productive route to creative success.

INTERVIEW WITH EMMA DONOGHUE ON MOTHERHOOD AND WRITING

Carolyn Jess-Cooke: Emma, your work deals profoundly with motherhood. Your novel *Room* (Little, Brown, 2010) has been called 'a hymn to motherhood', and certainly one of the reasons that I absolutely adored this book was because of the portrayal of Jack's mother – she was so fiercely protective of him, right down to the way she insisted on no more than 30 minutes of TV a day, and her prolonged nursing seemed as much as an act of comfort and nutrition as it did to protect against pregnancy. These details made the book an absolute joy for me! Can you talk about your inspiration for the portrait of motherhood in this book?

Emma Donoghue: Ma in Room was based more on my mother than on me (cheerful, solid, apparently tireless as she raised the eight of us), with a bit of playfulness taken from my relationship with my own kids. A friend who breastfed hers till five was an inspiration too. I have to ruefully admit that *Room* taught me that I know how to be a pretty perfect mother - the crafts, the games, the even-temperedness – I just can't do it. I'm one of those mothers in Starbucks that Jack notices, shutting up their kids with giant cookies so they can chat to friends (or in my case, get a scene written).

Carolyn: There's an assumption that motherhood is a terrible obstacle to female writers – indeed, there's an oft-used phrase that each child 'costs' a female writer four books – yet many women say that motherhood has energised and enhanced their creativity (and occasionally their productivity!). Have you found this? What challenges has it brought?

Emma: Wow, I'd only heard it as 'every baby costs you a book,' not four books! In my case I wouldn't say motherhood has slowed down my rate of production at all, and it's actually been a huge source of inspiration: my last three novels have drawn on this subject and I'm now writing fiction for children (8–12-year-olds) as well. Motherhood makes me more driven, more efficient with my time, and more able to tell myself 'stop whining about being so busy, and meet that deadline'. However... I've been parenting under ideal circumstances. My kids have two mothers, and my partner got six months of parental leave from her university after the birth of each of them, so I never (even though I was giving birth and breastfeeding) had to stop writing for more than the first six weeks. Also, we've used daycare, first part-time, then full-time; I've never had to be home alone with one or two kids all day. Motherhood (as a way of life) means something very different if you have to do all or most of the work yourself, and I can quite see why it might be hard to combine with writing in that case.

Carolyn: Of your new novel, *The Wonder* (Little, Brown, 2016), you've said that 'I put into it much that I've learned from motherhood'. Can you say a little bit about that?

Emma: *The Wonder* contrasts the pathological relationship between Anna and her mother (who is invested in the idea of her daughter as a fasting saint) with the newly formed bond between Anna and her nurse Lib – who begins as a total stranger to her, with no biological or legal tie, from a contrasting background (English, middle-class, educated), assigned to surveil her. I was interested in dissecting the elements of motherhood and asking – Solomon-style – who is the real mother.

Carolyn: The idea of 'the pram in the hallway' sadly still seems relevant for female artists; indeed, the most common question I'm asked as a writer is 'how do you find time to write'? I've been interested in this question because I think there's something about particular kinds of work that seem incompatible with being a woman, or a mother. For instance, when I go to my day job (as a lecturer), no one asks me how I find the time, but when it comes to writing, there's an assumption that women have other priorities and that writing is easily sidelined. Do you have any sense that writing is still not conceived as 'women's work', much less work that a mother would be doing?

Emma: I don't get the 'how do you have time to write' question, perhaps because my productivity makes it very obvious that I must be writing full-time. But on tour I get the irritating 'Why haven't you brought the kids with you? / Who's looking after your kids now?' questions (which my sense is) only women get asked. I asked a male writer recently what questions men get and he supplied 'what kind of car do you drive?' – which I find hilarious.

Carolyn: During the Writing Motherhood tour Kate Long talked about one of her books that dealt with serious women's issues. Then she held up the cover, which was pale pink with wellies on the front. The point she was making that, very often, the publishing world dismisses women's writing as whimsical. Have you found this with your work? What do you think about the representation of mothers/motherhood in the publishing world?

Emma: No, I've never had a whimsical cover; the darkness of my storylines seems to protect me from that.

Carolyn: *Room* was made into a film – did you perceive any differences in the representation of mothers between the publishing and film industries?

Emma: Hmm, perhaps film industry people were a little more uneasy about showing breastfeeding (though our wonderful director Lenny Abrahamson insisted on keeping that in, if discreetly). We feared that the film would be received as 'about a woman/mother, and therefore minority interest', but the fact that we got so many awards (and a Best Picture Academy nomination) would suggest that we were unduly fearful.

Carolyn: During the Writing Motherhood tour, we found a lot of women in the audiences wanted to write about their experiences of motherhood but lacked confidence – often this was less to do with their writing abilities than the perception that motherhood is a boring subject. What advice would you give to anyone wanting to begin to write about their experience of being a mother?

Emma: I probably shared that perception (motherhood as boringly generic) in that when our first child was born it didn't occur to me to write about my experience. But then when he was four I was seized with the idea for *Room*. I soon realized that the weird premise (young woman has to raise a child in a locked room) would allow me to pour all my thoughts and questions about parenting into a story which would defamiliarize the subject, literally isolating it in a spotlight. So my advice, I suppose, would be: this is fascinating stuff, but you need to find a fresh way of presenting it. As with human life in general.

MOTHERS & OTHERS

Greta Stoddart

AT THE SCHOOL GATES

I've come late
to the company of mothers,

this talk of sleep
and vaccinations,

this love they say
that'd lead them to kill.

I don't feel it
but am coming closer,

am being drawn
by a simple kinship

of hours kept:
morning bell, hometime.

I approach the gates
overcome with –

I don't know
what it is to belong

to any such group
or what to say.

Certainly not this:
that I feel like some creature

who was once driven out
because of some weakness

but who must return now
because she has young of her own

to the herd gathered here
at the edge of their territory.

Two policemen stand
in the middle of the playground.

It's dark this afternoon.
The woman's breath is a kind of light;

they don't look up or make room
but something closes in around me.

Kathryn Maris

SCHOOL RUN

I board the same bus I boarded that morning
and see the same driver from the earlier journey.
Our eyes meet; he remembers me too.
When I exit, I feel abandoned by this driver

I know from those many morning journeys
to my daughter's school in northwest London.
Why do I feel the driver has abandoned me?
Has an imagined intimacy developed?

At my daughter's school in northwest London
were the usual mums and dads I greet
out of an imagined sense of intimacy
that has nothing to do with friendship.

Among the many mums and dads I greeted
out of politeness or something like fondness
that has nothing to do with friendship,
were business people and psychoanalysts.

Out of politeness or something like fondness,
I do not ask the driver why he left me.
He's not in the business of psychoanalysis;
it's not his job to say I miss my *daughter*,

that it was a loss when my daughter left
my body, when I met her eyes after her birth.
It is not his place to say I'm losing my daughter.
I exit the same bus I boarded that morning.

Louisa Adjoa Parker

HIS KHAKI HOOD

A woman with a baby
in a backpack stops me
in the street when it's just
begun to rain and hail
and the sky is bright
the way a child's eyes
glitter darkly when
they are about to cry. She says
Excuse me, can you put his hood up?
So I lift the hood of her
baby's khaki coat gently
around his head; I love
this woman for not being afraid
to stop a stranger in the street
and ask them to help her keep
her little boy's head dry in the rain.

ja Smits (the pen-name I use for my writing and art). I work to the
first' principle, which perhaps makes it look as though I'm not
y 'doing work' but of course, outside of family time I'm very busy
ork (and I've learned that efficiency is key to making sure I get the
ry work done). However, that said, I know that this is a common
n asked of mothers who are doing a lot, and I think that this ques-
obably tells us more about the questioner's own sense of what they
and how *they* fill their time, rather than anything else. I first and
st value time with my family, but my publishing work and cre-
ork is also incredibly important to me, so it's a constant juggling
one that I (mainly) enjoy!

n: What kind of books do you publish?
I do 'mixed form' publishing, which means that I publish poetry,
and non-fiction for children and adults. Quite a range! But every
ays true to our remit: to publish books that celebrate femininity
pathy, with a view to normalising breastfeeding. The books that I
may not necessarily be about breastfeeding, but when breastfeed-
key element of the book (or story), it'll be written about in a
, though positive way.

a: How has the publishing world changed since you started out?
I'm not entirely sure if the publishing world has changed that
nce 2011. E-books, of course, and self-publishing are the new big
but actually, in many ways, the status quo remains. The lack of
y, and sexism, in publishing continue to be the two big issues
course, there's now the threat of Brexit) but the traditional pub-
seem to be slow to actually do anything about these issues.
er, it seems to me that the nimble and forward-thinking indie pub-
re the ones who are creating positive change. The indie sector is
ly where it's at...

a: Do you think motherhood as a subject is contentious?
guess that motherhood is a contentious subject, but that's only
every mother will experience motherhood differently and so
going to be differences of viewpoints. The labels: bad mother,
other, don't help either! It takes empathy and clear communica-
be able to truly connect with another human being, so if that's
from the 'motherhood narrative' then clearly, there's going to be
erstandings and disagreements. Also, children are not just

Stav Poleg

AT THE GALLERY OF MODERN ART

Again I'm late and this is only
coffee. You look night-pale and I am starved

for sleep.
            We had to meet– it's been too long–

but look at us–
you're holding onto a skinny latte, my

sentences collapse.   It's a hangover
                after no party. Just wakeful,

  yellow
    hours.

                                Look
how giving birth has left us deconstructed,

like Frank Gehry's Guggenheim,
                like Picasso's

Girl with a –   Where
                    were

we?
You need to go

        in ten,   I'm deep
                    into a cake. Still–

there's hope.
            Even Woody Allen's 'back on form'

                    with an anti-heroine
channeling Blanche DuBois. Remember

when we watched
        that Site-Specific Streetcar

at The Fringe?
                        I'm thinking

of a cappuccino reservoir,
              an extra shot espresso–

                              something,
                      but then you say

      Stav
              Stav!   Are you   OK?

I'm not.
I haven't had 3-hours' sleep

              in more than sixteen months.
                        'Another coffee?'

The waitress wears her weight
                      tucked in pink-pale

      skinny jeans.
        Have you seen Louise Bourgeois'

              sculpture at the Tate? You say,
a steel-and-marble female spider–

              huge as a three-mast ship–
      her soaring–

              slender legs encircling
      a sac

of eggs. She's
      there– she's not quite there– she's

              always ready and
                              awake.

You know what the artist named it?
                        'Maman.'

INTERVIEW WITH TEIKA BELL
ON MOTHERHOOD AND
PUBLISHING

Carolyn Jess-Cooke: Tell me a little about your publi
Mother's Milk Books.
Teika Bellamy: I set up Mother's Milk Books in 2011, wh
child had just turned one, so that I could publish an
Musings on Mothering that would raise funds for t
support charity, La Leche League GB. I wanted to make
had an ISBN, and that it would be available to buy thro
independent bookshops and gift shops, so it seemed li
it to have a 'traditional' publisher behind it (rather than
company). Also, back then, you couldn't buy single IS
plunge and bought a set of ten, with the vague idea
Mothering was a success (and if I enjoyed the publishi
could go on to publish other books. I learned so much
through that first book (I had no previous knowledge
basically I'm a self-taught publisher! However, since I
in science (I have a Ph.D. in Chemistry) and education
secondary level) I knew I had the necessary transferat
on a new career. And of course, all my years of being a
helped too!

Carolyn: What role did becoming a mother play
company?
Teika: Well, if I hadn't become a mother I don't th
Books would exist, because motherhood gave me a v
tive on life! Becoming a mother brought me so mu
course, there were challenges too. And I have the v
met through La Leche League GB to thank for helpin
challenges.

Carolyn: Do you get asked 'how do you find the tim
Teika: Actually, no, I don't often get asked this que
either know that I run a publishing company or they
Dr Teika Bellamy who runs Mother's Milk Books
who does the school run and bakes cakes and wh
willing to play games or help out at school. And so

important to their mothers and fathers but to the whole of society, so in a sense we're all invested in each other's children. So how well they are mothered and fathered is important to us all (which is probably why we're all so quick to judge others' parenting styles).

Carolyn: What would you change about the way we represent or talk about motherhood in literature?

Teika: I would definitely like to see more realistic portrayals of motherhood in literature – rather than just the stereotypes of 'good mother' and 'bad mother'. But also – obviously! – I would like to see more breastfeeding in children's books, because if children see that breastfeeding is the 'norm' for us humans – mammals – then those children will (hopefully) become adults that aren't outraged or shocked by this age-old way of feeding our babies, and they'll see it as something that will be part of their future.

Kathryn Simmonds

MEMORIAL

Early November in the market square
and you question me about the oversized poppies
in bloom overnight. I explain their purpose,
to make the town look pretty, and pull your hand tight
to prevent you from climbing the granite cross,
a memorial to those who were lost, and with them
their mothers, uncommemorated women
who lifted their hands wet from a sink, or span
at the knock and hurried to answer,
women whose bleeding had been done years before
in country hospitals, or bedrooms with the world shut out,
who had already given themselves up
to the mess of a shocked and howling child.

Jo Young

THE LADY STANDARD-BEARER FROM THE BRITISH LEGION

Like me she is skirted,
her knees freezing in the brittle
breath of November.

I hold the salute in a uniform which fitted
before breastfeeding sentences
condemned me to bulge from leather cross-belts
and gabardine routine.

The Last Post sounds and my angled elbow
aches as she lowers her standard.
Her colleague with the Union Jack,
who should know this better,
spies her movement and copies.
I sense that her petite, insistent dignity ruffles him.

Reveille cries out and the Legion men
huddle around her like toddlers
granting her a hesitant role
as captain of their haphazard ceremony.
I try a Sandhurst trick to nurse blood into my glutes
but she seems free of any urge to fidget.

Her children were brushed and liberty-bodiced,
they waited to get down and were grateful for bananas.
How we meet our children must be
the manner in which we greet all missions.
                          That, I see.

My gaze is on the creamy memorial ahead.
Amongst the men I spot Mary and below her
                          an Edith.

I wonder at these limestone women,
and at *her*   my veteran mother.
I yearn for her regimental poise, that maternal grace.

We share a glance and a tiny smile.

Carol Ann Duffy

WATER

Your last word was *water*,
which I poured in a hospice plastic cup, held
to your lips – your small sip, half-smile, sigh –
then, in the chair beside you,
                                        fell asleep.

Fell asleep for three lost hours,
only to waken, thirsty, hear then see
a magpie warn in a bush outside –
dawn so soon – and swallow from your still-full cup.

Water. The times I'd call as a child
for a drink, till you'd come, sit on the edge
of the bed in the dark, holding my hand,
just as we held hands now and you died.

A good last word.
                        Nights since I've cried, but gone
to my own child's side with a drink, watched
her gulp it down then sleep. *Water*.
What a mother brings
                                through darkness still
to her parched daughter.

Rachel Richardson

TRANSMISSION

There was a girl who heard it happen:
Amelia Earhart calling
on the radio, she and her navigator
alternately cursing and defining their position
by latitude, as best they could read it
in the bellowing wind, and by what
they could surmise of their rate per hour,
last land they'd seen. *Stay with me, someone,*
and the girl wrote each word
in her composition book, kept the channel
tuned, hunched to the receiver
when static overtook the line.
Why do I think of her?
The coast guard laughed at her father
holding out the schoolgirl scrawl
and sent him home ashamed. A lost woman
is a lost woman, he told her, and the sea
is dark and wide.

Emma McKervey

PATAGONIA

I have read there is a tribe living in the mountains
and lakes of Patagonia who can barely count beyond five,
yet have a language so precise there is a word for;
the curious experience of unexpectedly discovering
something spherical and precious in your mouth,
formed perhaps by grit finding its way into the shellfish
(such as an oyster) you have just eaten.
Or something like that. I identify with this conceptual position.
And as I listen to my children debate on the train
as to which is the greater – googolplex or infinity –
whilst knowing they still struggle with their 4 times table,
I can't help but reflect that maybe we should be
on a small canoe at great altitude, trailing
our semantic homespun nets behind instead.

Laura Kasischke

GAME

I thought we were playing a game
in a forest that day.
I ran as my mother chased me.

But she'd been stung by a bee.
Or bitten by a snake.
She shouted my name, which

even as a child I knew was not
'Stop. Please. I'm dying.'

I ran deeper
into the bright black trees
happily
as she chased me: How

lovely the little bits and pieces.
The fingernails, the teeth. Even
the bombed cathedrals
being built inside of me.

How sweet
the eye socket. The spine. The
curious, distant possibility that God
had given courage
to human beings
that we might
suffer a little longer.

And by the time

I was willing to admit that
all along
all along
I'd known it was no game

I was a grown woman, turning
back, too late.

Jackie Wills

GIYA'S MAPS

My daughter closes the door to her room,
pins on a note: '*No Jackies*'. I knock
but she won't open, screams: '*Go away!*'
and I stand on the stairs, summoning up
mornings she's walked from her bed
to ours, hair tangled around her face,
announced by a loose floorboard in the hall.
She brings her warmth and sleep,
slides back into both as she squeezes
between us, arms flung out and kicks us
to the sides until one of us gives in
and traces her steps to the space she's left
by a pink cushion, dolls without heads,
hairbands, loose beads: a tourist
in this island of hers, unsure of the geography
but trying to read the map of roads
and bridleways, directions she leaves
in notes around the house. Her territory's
marked out in lists, of best friends, love
letters, apologies, '*I hate mum*' copied out
five times. I stand outside her door
with the other Jackies; know I shouldn't disturb
her as she draws her maps, feathered
coastlines with bays named after cats.
There's *Claire's Accessories* and *Butlins*.
I have scraps of these maps in my purse,
sometimes find one in a notebook,
halfway through. One day she'll come across them
as I do, in the treasure box with tags
from her newborn wrists, milk teeth, school reports.
She'll visit those places again, maybe remember
me outside the door calling: 'Please let me in.'

Wendy Videlock

FLOWERS

for my mother

They are fleeting.
They are fragile.
They require

little water.
They'll surprise you.
They'll remind you

that they aren't
and they are you.

INTERVIEW WITH SARAH MOSS ON MOTHERHOOD AND WRITING

November 2016

Carolyn Jess-Cooke: A lot of female writers have commented that motherhood enhanced their artistic creation and productivity, and that despite often not having time to write, a creative output became vital after having children. How would you say motherhood affects your own writing? Does it enhance it, or bring challenges to it? How did you deal with those challenges?

Sarah Moss: I had my first child at 26, very young by the standards of my peers. I'd just started a post-doctoral research fellowship, so my writing practice developed with my maternity rather than being interrupted by it. I grew up with the idea that women create: my mother was always designing and making textiles, my grandmother was a teacher, so although nobody else was much interested in writing it was normal to me that a woman who was pushing a pram or chopping an onion was also thinking about some kind of making. I always had a little time to write. There are photos of me with a baby asleep on my chest and a laptop on my lap, and an insane photo of me sitting on the grass breastfeeding an infant propped on my elbow while using my hands to type while a four-year-old rides a tricycle in the background. (With hindsight and maturity, I regret some of these moments. The book could have waited a few months.) I stayed in full-time academic work all the way through and I have a useful ability to remain functional with very little sleep.

Carolyn: I found that I read poems and essays by women about motherhood with an intensity and heightened understanding. For instance, I'm now slightly obsessed with sleep and therefore felt a huge compassion for Anna in your novel *Night Waking* (Granta, 2012). Do you think your motherhood triggered a similar shift in reading and/or engaging with language?

Sarah: Yes, but absolutely the other way! The books I read while breastfeeding were far more blokey than my usual diet. I read the sort of men's travel writing I'd usually dismiss as nostalgic and narcissistic, and lots of Conrad and Updike, dead white men of finely-turned sentences and troubling politics. I'm sure it was straightforward denial on my part, but I also felt that my life had been taken over by meconium and mastitis and if I didn't have to be thinking about body fluids I wasn't going to. I was similarly resistant to those conversations and used to seek out the women at mother-and-baby groups who would talk about work or books or politics or pretty much anything except babies. I would never have gone to live in isolation with young children because I knew exactly how much I depended on nursery and urban infrastructure to remain approximately functional. When I wrote *Night Waking*, my youngest child had started school, both kids were sleeping at night and my husband had been the primary carer for several years. I could revisit the poo and sleep deprivation from a place of relative safety.

Carolyn: You capture motherhood and parenthood brilliantly, particularly in *The Tidal Zone* (Granta, 2016) where (the first literary?) stay-at-home dad, Adam, offers a pretty fabulous balancing act of domestic duties. The novel focuses on his viewpoint, rather than his wife Emma's, and I found myself applauding the novel the whole way through for this. Why was it important to represent a man as the primary caregiver/washer of socks?

Sarah: It wasn't really a political decision, it was just the way the book came. Adam's was the voice I found. But I had often been frustrated by modern discourses around caring and sock-washing because among my friends and colleagues as well as in my marriage, the men of my generation are changing nappies, washing socks and getting up in the night, and that labour seems to be utterly invisible.

Carolyn: I love the reference of 'the pram in the hallway' early on in *Night Waking* where you suggest that a woman behind a pram becomes unrecognizable, if not invisible. Why do you think that is?

Sarah: At the time I thought it was because it simply doesn't cross most people's minds that the person propelling the pushchair might have any other function in life, but we should bear in mind that my own experience of prams was while I was a junior member of staff in a deeply conservative enclave of a deeply conservative institution that dominated the city where I lived. It was a revelation to have a second child while at the University of Kent and find procreation was a normal and happy thing to do rather than a shameful betrayal of the life of the mind, and I think there my friends and colleagues usually did see me behind the pram. Students didn't, but that was OK.

Carolyn: The idea of 'the pram in the hallway' still seems relevant for female artists; indeed, the most common question I'm asked as a writer is 'how do you find time to write'? Male writers with children don't seem to be asked this question. What's your view on that?

Sarah: I get asked that all the time too and it makes me cross! If I dare, I say 'it's interesting that we don't ask men that question'. If I don't dare, I say 'my partner is the primary carer and the kids are old enough to respect my work'. There's still a popular idea that women's work, and especially women's creative practice, is a form of self-indulgence that must never be allowed to interfere with childcare or housework while male writers are bards attended by muses.

Carolyn: The other angle to this question is that, as an academic, I never get asked 'how do you find time to go to work?' Women may get asked how they juggle their careers with children, but there's something about art and writing that seems socially incompatible with motherhood. Anne Tyler touches upon it in her essay 'Still Just Writing', which she wrote in response to people asking if she was *still just writing*. Likewise, Cyril Connolly's description of 'the pram in the hallway' was directed at men, because of course a woman with a child wouldn't be writing at all. Do you think writing is still not conceived as 'women's work', much less work that a mother would be doing?

Sarah: I don't know. My conversations with male writer friends suggest that writing is often perceived as no job for a real man, which would seem to imply that it's a girly pursuit, but I imagine the inflections are more complicated than a gender binary. At least in England everything is always as much about class as gender, and writing is perhaps a bourgeois pursuit. We're living in an anti-intellectual moment where anyone who's paid to think is probably a traitor, male or female.

Carolyn: During the Writing Motherhood tour Kate Long talked about one her books that dealt with serious women's issues. Then she held up the cover, which was pale pink with wellies on the front. The point she was making that, very often, the publishing world dismisses women's writing as whimsical. Have you found this with your work? What do you think about the representation of mothers/motherhood in the publishing world?

Sarah: There are very many reasons why I feel extremely lucky to be published by Granta, and this is one of them. No-one ever suggested pink frilly covers, and I've always been consulted about every aspect of book design. I know my editor has sometimes rejected cover images for exactly this reason without even telling me. But that is unusual, and I always find it strange that a society which continues to blame parents for everything also regards the discussion of parenthood as trivial, a minority interest. Parents, after all, are the one thing we have all had.

Carolyn: The idea of the 'mother' is so politically charged, and I found it difficult to accept the preconceptions that came with it. For instance, I'm still not sure what a 'stay at home mother' is, or a 'working mother', despite having technically been both. Have you found your ideas of motherhood and being a mother changing over time? Do they still inform your work?

Sarah: The categories are ideological and inevitably hierarchical. No one talks about 'working fathers', though I found when writing *The Tidal Zone* that it's hard to find a phrase to describe the situation of the man who chooses to make unpaid domestic labour his primary occupation. (House-husband? Stay-at-home-dad? They all sound ironic, though maybe no more so than the female equivalents.) My experience is that the 'idea of motherhood' becomes much less monolithic as everyone gets older, and 'being a mother' becomes more obviously a relationship like any other than a site of social conflict. The mother I am now is far more the product of my own personhood and that of my kids than the performance of a socially defined role. I'm sure those relationships do inform my writing, but as much in giving me intimate knowledge of other perspectives than in making me want to report on motherhood. Of course I don't and never can see the world through my kids' eyes, but I see more of it than I would if I were not a parent.

TRANSITIONS

Kate Long

THE FIVE STAGES OF MOTHERHOOD

1   1996 – A Safe Place

I have my eyes tight-shut so I cannot see his face. His hands are moving across my belly, pressing and kneading at the flesh. For a moment he takes away his fingers, and then replaces them on the inside of my thighs, pressing down gently. I let myself fall open to him because what else is there to do? I'm exposed, I'm all his. If he'll only speak to me. If only he'll tell me what I need to hear. There is a long moment. At last I hear the doctor sigh. 'Mrs Long, I don't think this pregnancy's going very well.'

So begins the first of my three miscarriages. Initially when I confide in friends and family, they're reassuring. As the months go on, however, and it's bad news upon bad news, I feel they're losing faith. I'm letting everyone down. I become depressed. I develop eczema on my scalp. My confidence in the fairness of life drains away. Babies are everywhere, granted to the deserving and undeserving alike.

I give away the baby clothes I've collected, and start to write. This seems to help me get through the darkest days. In my story I create a world where I have complete control over the scope and pace of events, and there are no nasty surprises waiting round the corner. My heroine is ultimately safe because I'm there to guard her. Whatever I want comes to pass. Soon this story-world becomes my escape. This novel I'm writing now will not be published, but it keeps me sane, which for the time being is more important.

2   2001 – Exhaustion

When I squint at the digital clock it says 2am. The baby is crying and must be comforted, but I know that if my toddler hears me moving about, he'll call for me too. I have not slept a whole night through for three years. In six hours' time I know I'll have to be dropping both boys at nursery, then driving 20 miles to the school where I teach GCSE English. There I will have to try and hide from my students the fact that my eyes are too bleary to focus and that my blood is turned to coffee.

Yet somehow each evening, after the marking and planning are done, I work on a new novel. It's become a habit I can't leave alone. My writing might be moving forward at a snail's pace, I might have to begin each session by clearing Lego from off my keyboard, but actually I am making progress. Like dieting, with which I am also struggling: even the tiniest increments mount up. Some days all I do is add a single sentence. That's fine. It's not a race. As long as I get there in the end.

I often meet people who say, 'Yeah, I'd write a novel myself if I ever had the time.' I want to hit them over the head with a piece of Tomy train track.

3.   2006 – I, the Bad Mother

'So tell us, in what ways are YOU a shoddy parent?' asks the journalist. I've started to get this question a lot. It's my own fault: I would appear to have published a definitive guide on the subject. Some bookshop customers glance at the title and assume it's an instruction manual. So I cast about for my failings and 'fess up – I rely too much on processed food, I'm over-anxious, I repeatedly lose letters from school so my kids are the only ones who arrive not in fancy dress or pyjamas or sporting red plastic noses on the critical day.

Then again, I tell the journalist, isn't motherhood too complex and nuanced a job not to make mistakes? It's inevitable. Guilt is the mantle we have to wear. We just need to keep trying our best, and listening to our children, and forgiving ourselves when we fall short of the mark. *The Bad Mother's Handbook* says to the reader, 'We're all struggling, every last one of us. Modern life is insanely busy, and tough. But you know what? You're a pretty good mum, on the scale of things, and you should be proud of what you've achieved. High five.'

4   2011 – The Daughters I Shall Never Have

I've been incredibly lucky. Life has gifted me two beautiful boys. They are healthy, clever, kind, funny and one of them is already taller than me. After those miserable early miscarriages I suffered, I now feel like the most privileged mother in the world.

And yet I wonder what kind of a mum I'd have been to girls. Ours is a house of shaving equipment, huge pairs of discarded trainers, Lynx body spray. What if I'd had daughters instead of sons, though? How might they have turned out? Would they have been the outdoorsy type like me, scrambling around in muddy trousers, pursuing moths and newts? Would they have been neat and fashion-conscious, tech-savvy, urban? Would we have shared a special, arcane female understanding, or clashed horribly? I'll never know. That chance is gone.

But the magic of books is that they allow you to travel the paths you didn't take. So in fact I do have daughters. I have spiky, over-anxious Charlotte, who thinks she knows better than her mum and consequently gets herself into one pickle after another. I have shy, overweight, bisexual Kat and spoilt, angry Jasmine. As their creator, I am allowed to chide these young women, and make them pay for their rash actions; conversely, I feel proud of them when they learn from their mistakes and behave with courage and dignity. When Freya finally confronts her useless boyfriend, I'm standing on the sidelines, cheering. I'm thrilled that Kat manages to get to university after all her social difficulties. These are girls I've formed and guided, and they live on in my head. I think I make a tender Imaginary Mother.

5   2014 – What is a Mother?

One of my earliest memories is of my own mum telling me, 'You're special because we went out and *chose* you.' I was adopted in 1965, the day of Winston Churchill's funeral, with the shipyard cranes along the Thames dipping in salute. So I understood right from the start, my birth mother was a different person from the one bringing me up. How did that make me feel? Proud, reassured. Entirely wanted. Sometimes, in private, I fantasized a bit about my possible genetic background, but it was idle speculation, the early novelist toying with a narrative idea. What I mainly felt towards my birth mum was intense gratitude that she'd been selfless enough to give me up. What courage that must have taken.

Over the years, I've come to appreciate that the title 'Mother' is not an automatic right, it's something earned daily. My mum was my mum by virtue of all the nights she sat up with me in illness or after a bad dream; by virtue of those books we read together, the times she stopped what she was doing to help with my homework, the walks we took, the tears she mopped. I can't believe I could have been loved more even if I'd been biologically hers. So adoption is a theme I've returned to again and again in my books, and championed. Karen discovers in her thirties that she's adopted and feels compelled to reclaim her 'other life', but finds it isn't the bed of roses she'd imagined. Freya's loyalties are torn between Melody, her birth mother, and Liv, her adoptive mum, both of whom compete for her attention, but in the end they all three come together in support of each other.

In these days of blended families, many of us are bringing up children who aren't our own, and most of us are doing a splendid job. I always wanted my books to wave a flag for those crowds of ordinary mothers who simply try their best, whatever their background, blood-relationship, or qualifications. If I've made even one reader feel better about herself, then I'm happy.

Julie Hogg

BORROWING YOU BACK

This Summer, I've mostly been
losing you bit by bit. Carefully
loosening grips I hope were
judged well and time will tell
in all of those elusive revelations
to lucky those who love you too.

That girl in the car-park, yellow
sundress, yellow filigree lantern,
delicate white sandals and fine
sunflower clip in her wavy hair,
we both knew that she was you.

The boy on the beach, how his
Dad humbly crumpled when he
splashed his honed muscles and
simultaneously saw compassion.

When you were in Notting Hill I
lay on your bed and remembered
you radiantly alighting at stations.

Growing into own, arms around
shoulders. Look, look how good
enough I am.

Borrowing you back by listening,
just listening,

listening
like

luxury.

Emma Simon

PLAIT

The trick is to hold three braids in two hands
and ignore the logistics of mornings.
Wind the first over the second, then cross

the third over the first, and so on. Don't get cross
as arguments slip like hoarded minutes out of hand.
Flex zen-calmed fingers: remember even school mornings

don't last forever. Focus on this Tuesday morning:
soft nape and collar crease, the wonky plait. Let its criss cross
weave a tender magic, like a proverb handed

across generations, mourning there is not enough time, but
    just enough hands

Jane McKie

ARCHIPELAGO

My husband levitates at night: birds begin
to vibrate, snow sifts from the curtains,
and I wake to see him lift an inch, cat-curled
on his side, soft as bread. He faces away
but I can tell he smiles, every breath huffs
upwards. I don't touch him. I fear his rest,
worry my stranger's reach will stop his heart.

My mother searches drawers at night: thunk
thunk – I know they're empty, the next room
made hollow with the slap of resinless MDF,
its peculiar Calvinism. What does she look for?
Not folded vests, broderie anglaise, not scalloped
necks or figure-hugging skirts; she prefers
pantsuits these days, the shed skins of shapes.

My daughter lines her tired eyes at night: violet
or ultramarine, even when she stays at home.
I can hear the tinny iPod dreaming, its tsking
irks me like no other sound – insectoid,
subtly overbearing. At least she's here.
It makes me wince, finding a vein in my head,
but it tsk tsk tsks my melancholy girl to sleep.

My son is like my husband at night: lost
to the pillow without complications.
The book he reads behind his lids might shock me.
I choose not to enquire – of myself, or of friends
with famished boys. It is enough to know
his hair smells like pan-drops, his lovely feet
slop over the bed. He is an open lotus flower.

Fiona Benson

EUROFIGHTER TYPHOON

My daughters are playing outside with a plastic hoop;
the elder is trying to hula, over and over,
but the hoop falls off her hips, too heavily freighted with beads,
it's over-accessorised junk, but she keeps trying
and the younger is watching and giggling,
and they're happy in the bright afternoon.
I'm indoors at the hob with the door open
so I can see them, because the elder might trip,
and the younger is still a baby and liable to eat dirt,
when out of clear skies a jet comes in low
over the village. At the first muted roar
the elder runs in squealing then stops in the kitchen,
her eyes adjusting to the dimness, looking foolish
and unsure. I drop the spoon and bag of peas
and leave her frightened and tittering, wiping my hands
on my jeans, trying to walk and not run,
because I don't want to scare the baby
who's still sat on the patio alone, looking for her sister,
bewildered, trying to figure why she's gone –
all this in the odd, dead pause of the lag –
then sound catches up with the plane
and now its grey belly's right over our house
with a metallic, grinding scream
like the sky's being chain-sawed open
and the baby's face drops to a square of pure fear,
she tips forward and flattens her body on the ground
and presses her face into the concrete slab.
I scoop her up and she presses in shuddering,
screaming her strange, *halt* pain cry
and it's all right now I tell her again and again,
but it's never all right now – Christ have mercy –
my daughter in my arms can't steady me –
always some woman is running to catch up her children,
we dig them out of the rubble in parts like plaster dolls –
Mary Mother of God have mercy, mercy on us all.

Tina Chang

MILK

Milk in the batter! Milk in the batter! We bake cake! And nothing's the matter!
                    – *In the Night Kitchen,* Maurice Sendak

In every definition of home, my son conjures milk.
The sun as milk, milk spills through open
doorways, bed of warm milk, face of milk,
milk trousers, a truck full of milk. A milky light
passes through the lens of my camera.

All of his young life, my son thought of milk,
and he asked for it each night. In every memory
I have of him, his hands are outstretched
and he is asking for his last bottle.
In every version of a life, I never refuse him.

On the television, the nation listens to the story
of Leiby Kletzky. Today, I think of his mother
who waited for him, allowing him for the first time
to walk home alone. In that definition of home,
the boy promised to walk one straight line

until he reached his front door. That morning,
he held a key, heavy and shining, made especially
for him. In the ancient story of boys, he headed up
the street past the lone dog barking near the fire hydrant,
past the circle of children careening into their own shadows.

And in the ancient story of boys, he walked through
his front door and this was his right of passage.
He placed his book bag on the coffee table,
and the boy and the mother sat together
in the large reading chair, in the living room light.

But this version isn't true.

Tonight, I hold my son closer. As I put on his night
clothes, I'm afraid of the world. I find all the stories
horrifying. In the book of nursery rhymes the old woman
sends her son to bed without food, a king beats
a knave for stealing pies, and the dog cannot find his bone,

though he runs in circles day after day. Perhaps
if I rewrite all the old stories, a new era will begin.
Era of the Forgiven. Era of Redemption. Era
of Safekeeping. Tonight Milk stains my blouse,
love so deep, it runs from me. After the old stories

are finished, my son says, *The story, again.* I open
the book. The owls lift from the pages. The lake
is a bowl of nightmilk. And this, a place so safe,
we are weightless, buoyant in its murky sweetness.
Free from a promise that each new day startles us alive.

* Note: Leiby Kletzky, an eight-year-old Hasidic Jewish boy, was kid-
napped while walking home from day camp on June 11, 2011. His body was
found two days later in the Kensington, New York apartment of Levi Aron
and also in a dumpster in Sunset Park. Leiby had begged his parents to
walk home alone instead of taking the school bus. His parents honored his
wish after practicing the route home many times. Upon leaving camp, he
missed a turn and headed in the wrong direction.

Deborah J. Bennett

LAUNDRY

Quiet, these nights. Perched on the satin spread
quilted and draped over the corner of the bed,

queen-sized. She plants her feet, picks tiny socks
like beans off the trellis. Spun cotton her cash crop

these days. She pairs them, folding the ankles
one over the other. Precision, care, the mantle

of motherhood. Perhaps an hour more before
the sidewall scrapes the curb cut, the heavy door

opens, the work boots stamp through shallow puddles,
brown pine needles. Drained amber bottles muddle

his thoughts. Still straddling a bar stool, he is safe
and so are they. Later, fists and spittle will strafe

walls, headboard, wife. Later, she will blot the blood
from the house dress. Later, scrub the grease and food

stains that radiate out, night-blooming. Now, the halo
of name brand bleach fills her nose. Now, bright rompers glow

under lamplight. Before she sleeps, she lines the hall
a basket for each child, fleet bracing for the squall.

Rhian Edwards

PARENTS' EVENING

We feel she may be cheating
at reading and spelling.
She has failed to grasp the planets
and the laws of science,
has proven violent in games
and fakes asthma for attention.

She is showing promise with the Odyssey,
has learned to darn starfish
and knitted a patch for the scarecrow.
She appears to enjoy measuring rain,
pretending her father is a Beatle
and insists upon your death
as the conclusion to all her stories.

Patricia Ace

FIRST BLOOD

The aubergine streaks
of my daughter's first blood
bubble up through soap suds
like an ending.

Two weeks a teenager,
the balloons from her birthday
still sagging, softened,
puckered at the window.
Now suddenly she's a woman,
her eggs ripe as redcurrants,
her ovaries plump as the plums
spilling their yellow harvest
on the late-summer lawn,
her breasts budding hard
as the small sharp apples in the yard,
her blood clear as cranberries.

A chill in the air ushers Autumn
as we freewheel on bikes through the wood.
The undergrowth lashes our ankles
the bite of nettles, the jag of brambles
pricking our skin.

She comes to me after the bike ride
a flush of colour on her cheekbones.
I'm slumped on the sofa like dough.
I buckle as if she's punched me,
winded, the air kneaded out of me.

Then I'm back in the hot August dawn
of the night she was born
squeezing my mother's hand
so hard she had to take her rings off
before they sliced the tender place
between her fingers,

seeing her shrink from my terrified gaze
as I gulped from the mask, drowning.
And when it was done, my mother staring
down at the little pink bundle and saying
One day she'll have to go through all this.

Here she stands, my girl, so tall
and proud I can hardly believe I bore her.
I want to throw my arms around her,
to bake her a cake with candles.

But I slope off to the bathroom instead
rummage in the cupboard for the towels
I've secretly stashed for this day,
slip her underwear into the sink,
watch the water blush
as the rosewood stain lifts.

The aubergine streaks
of my daughter's first blood
bubble up to the surface,
a beginning.

Natalie Shaw

HOW TO TELL YOUR SON HE HAS NO FRIENDS

You will get the first bit wrong: he won't
be able to meet your eye. In the dark,
you can hold his hand and stroke his hair.
Forget the things you said this morning.
Forget the things you said this morning.

Take him to the pool and swim
together. He'll start off scared, you can
take your time. Unwrap him gently,
hold him in the water. Together
you'll watch the water slap with light;

it will start to sparkle up
through your tummies; you can laugh,
first him, then you. Your cracked-up shells
are smoothing over, your scrambled bits
are safe inside again. Go back,

back in the dark to see his outline,
the shape of who he is, the gap
that spools and spools around his shadow.
Tell him it's your gap too, tell him,
tell him. Hear him breathe.

Ellen Phethean

YOUNGEST SON
LEAVES HOME

The house is a beach –
the tide's gone out
leaving it empty, liminal.
Littered along the strand,
pieces the sea didn't take.

The whole world is in flux:
telescopes penetrate deep space,
galaxies expand, universes multiply,
but the steady moon
pulls the sea
then lets go
as it should.

Rita Ann Higgins

GRANDCHILDREN

It's not just feasible at the moment
one daughter tells me.
What with Seamus still robbing banks
and ramming garda vans when he gets emotional
on a fish-free Friday in February.

Maybe the other daughter could deliver.
She thinks not, not at the moment anyway
while Thomas still has a few tattoos to get,
to cover any remaining signs that might link him
with the rest of us.

Just now a B52 bomber flies over
on its way from Shannon
to make a gulf in some nation's genealogy.

The shadow it places on all our notions is crystal clear
and for a split of a second helping
it juxtaposes the pecking order.
Now bank robbers and tattooers
have as much or as little standing
as popes and princes
and grandchildren become another lonely utterance
impossible to pronounce.

Brenda Shaughnessy

MAGI

If only you'd been a better mother.

How could I have been a better mother?
I would have needed a better self,
and that is a gift I never received.

So you're saying it's someone else's fault?

The gift of having had a better mother myself,
my own mother having had a better mother herself.
The gift that keeps on not being given.

Who was supposed to give it?

How am I supposed to know?

Well, how am I supposed to live?

I suppose you must live as if you had been
given better to live with. Comb your hair, for instance.

I cut off my hair, to sell for the money
to buy you what you wanted.

I wanted nothing but your happiness.

I can't give you that!
What would Jesus do?
He had a weird mother too . . .

Use the myrrh, the frankincense, as if
it were given unconditionally, your birthright.

It's a riddle.

All gifts are a riddle, all lives are
in the middle of mother-lives.

But it's always winter in this world.
There is no end to ending.

The season of giving, the season
when the bears are never cold,
because they are sleeping.

The bears are never cold, Mama,
but I am one cold, cold bear.

Catherine Ayres

TWO SONS IN A LAKE

Their bodies rise
from water into sky,

out of context in blue.
My little monoliths,

the camera's turned you to stone
and I search the space between us.

Youngest faces me,
his torso full of sun;

our ripples overlap, like soundwaves,
two notes in the same song.

Oldest boy is further out;
did I ask him, or did he decide

to stand on the point of turning
new shadows on his chest?

I want to swim back into shot
so our circles touch.

Behind him, distant pine,
the mountain in its own light.

Suzanna Fitzpatrick

FLEDGLINGS

I stroke the tiny kites
of your shoulder blades,
imagine wings. Gingerly

I stretch my own.
It's been so long
since I trusted them.

As your nestling's down
gives place to feathers,
I'll re-learn flight with you. Let's stand,

teeter-happy, brink-thrilled,
taste the wind. And we'll soar,
my darling. We will soar.

NOTES ON CONTRIBUTORS

Patricia Ace published *First Blood* with HappenStance in 2006. That year she started an MLitt in Creative Writing at Glasgow University for which she gained a Distinction in 2008. *Fabulous Beast* came out from Freight Books in 2013. Her work appears in *Be the First to Like This: New Scottish Poetry* (Vagabond Voices, 2014), *Hallelujah For 50ft Women: Poems about Women's Relationship to their Bodies* (Bloodaxe, 2015) and *Umbrellas of Edinburgh* (Freight Books, 2016). In 2017 she took part in a collaborative project and performance, run by The Poetry School, commemorating the centenary of the First World War. Patricia lives in rural Perthshire with her husband and has two grown-up daughters.

Louisa Adjoa Parker writes poetry, fiction and BAME history. Her first poetry collection, *Salt-sweat and Tears*, was published in 2007 by Cinnamon Press. Her pamphlet, *Blinking in the Light* was also published by Cinnamon in 2016. Her work has appeared in *Wasafiri, Envoi, Out of Bounds: British Black & Asian Poets*, and *Closure: Contemporary Black British Short Stories*. She has been highly commended by the Forward Prize, short-listed by the Bridport Prize and long-listed by the *Mslexia* Novel Competition. In 2016 Louisa received a grant from Arts Council England, and is working with mentors Jacob Ross and Jan Fortune on a third poetry collection, first novel and short story collection. Twitter: @LouisaAdjoa

Natalya Anderson is a poet and former ballet dancer from Toronto, Canada. She won the Bridport Prize in 2014 for her poem, 'Clear Recent History', and was one of four finalists for the 2015 Ballymaloe International Poetry Prize. Her poetry and feature writing have appeared in *Poetry London, Prac Crit, The Moth,* and elsewhere.

Mary Austin Speaker is a poet and book designer. Her first full-length collection, *Ceremony*, was selected by Matthea Harvey as winner of the 2012 Slope Editions book prize and was published in February 2013. Her second book, *The Bridge*, was published in January 2016 by Shearsman Books. Her work has appeared in recent issues of *Boston Review, Subtropics, Shifter,* and *Matter Monthly*. Together with Chris Martin and Sam Gould, she co-edits and designs *Society*, a new publication project about poetry and power. She lives in Minneapolis, Minnesota.

Janette Ayachi (b.1982) is a Scottish-Algerian poet who has been published in over sixty journals and anthologies from presses such as

Polygon, Freight and Salt's *The Best British Poetry of 2015*. She collaborates with artists, has been shortlisted for a few writerly accolades and has performed her work on BBC Radio as well as across the UK at various events. She has an MSc in Creative Writing from Edinburgh University, is the author of two poetry pamphlets and her children's chapter book *The Mermaid, The Girl and The Gondola* was published by Black Wolf Edition Press in 2016. She currently lives in Edinburgh with her two young daughters Aria and Lyra.

Catherine Ayres is a teacher from Northumberland. Her collection, *Amazon*, is published by Indigo Dreams.

Anna Barker is a journalist, novelist and academic writing consultant. Her first novel, *The Floating Island*, was published by Random House in 2008 and won the Society of Authors' Betty Trask Award for best debut from a writer under 35. *Before I Knew Him* followed a year later and was shortlisted for a Good Housekeeping Good Read award. She is currently juggling various projects for the Royal Literary Fund, writing her third novel, and completing her PhD by Publication in Creative Writing at Huddersfield University. She is single parent to an aspiring 7-year-old scientist/wizard.

Elizabeth Barrett is the author of four collections of poetry including *The Bat Detector* (Wrecking Ball Press, 2005) and *A Dart of Green and Blue* (Arc Publications, 2010). Her poetry is widely published in anthologies and magazines and she has been the recipient of a number of poetry prizes including an Arts Council of England Writers Award. Elizabeth lives in Sheffield where she works as a university lecturer in education.

Dr Teika Bellamy is the founder and managing editor of Mother's Milk Books. In 2015, Teika was the recipient of the Women in Publishing's New Venture Award for pioneering work on behalf of under-represented groups in society; Mother's Milk Books was also longlisted in the 2016 Saboteur Awards category 'Most Innovative Publisher'. Teika is a popular speaker who is passionate about the role of independent presses and women authors within the publishing world. When she's not busy with the press, or her family, she's busy writing or creating art under her pen-name, Marija Smits. www.mothersmilkbooks.com

Deborah J. Bennett's poems and translations have appeared in *Salamander, Artlines 2* and *FUSION*. She was also recently named a finalist in *Southwest Review's* Morton Marr Poetry Contest. Her latest essay, on sleep inequality, appeared on *Cognoscenti*. Deborah teaches at Berklee College of Music and lives with her family in Boston.

Fiona Benson lives in rural Devon with her husband James Meredith and their daughters, Isla and Rose. She received an Eric Gregory Award in 2006, and was a participant in the Faber New Poets programme in 2009 with the pamphlet *Faber New Poets 1*. Her first full-length collection *Bright Travellers* (Jonathan Cape, 2014) won the Seamus Heaney Prize for first collection and the Geoffrey Faber Memorial Prize, and was shortlisted for the T.S. Eliot prize, amongst others.

Kaddy Benyon's first collection, *Milk Fever*, won the Crashaw Prize and was published by Salt in 2012. She is also a Granta New Poet and has recently completed a residency at The Polar Museum in Cambridge where she wrote and is currently editing her second collection, *Call Her Alaska*.

Liz Berry lives in Birmingham with her family. Her debut collection *Black Country* (Chatto, 2014) was a Poetry Book Society Recommendation, received a Somerset Maugham Award, won the Geoffrey Faber Memorial Prize and the Forward Prize for Best First Collection 2014.

Sujata Bhatt was born in India. She grew up in India and in the USA. Her most recent books are *Collected Poems* (PBS Special Commendation, 2013) and *Poppies in Translation* (PBS Recommendation, 2015). She has received numerous awards including the Commonwealth Poetry Prize (Asia) and a Cholmondeley Award. In 2014 she was the first recipient of the Mexican International Poetry Prize, *Premio Internacional de Poesía Nuevo Siglo de Oro 1914–2014*. Her work has been widely anthologised, broadcast on radio and television, and has been translated into more than twenty languages. She divides her time between Germany and elsewhere.

Kate Bingham is the author of two novels, several screenplays and three collections of poetry. *Quicksand Beach* was short-listed for the Forward Prize, Best Collection, in 2006, and in 2010 'On Highgate Hill' was short-listed for the Forward Prize, Best Single Poem. Her third collection is *Infragreen* ('full of sensuous, imaginative and beautifully accomplished work', *Poetry Review*) and her most recent work can be found in 'Five Poems', a leaflet published by Clutag Press.

Zoë Brigley is the author of two books of poems. *The Secret* was listed for the Dylan Thomas Prize for International Writers Under 30 Years Old and was made a UK Poetry Book Society Recommendation (Bloodaxe, 2007). *Conquest* was also a UK Poetry Book Society Recommendation (Bloodaxe, 2012). She also edited the academic volume, *Feminism, Literature and Rape Narratives* (Routledge 2010). Her writing has appeared in such publications as *Women's Studies Quarterly*, *Poetry Review*, *Calyx*,

The Platte Valley Review, Poetry Ireland Review, The Times Higher Education Supplement and *Frontiers: A Journal of Women's Studies*. She has received an Eric Gregory Award from the Society of Authors in London as well as a Welsh Academy Bursary and she won the English Association Poetry Fellows' Prize.

Jane Burn is a writer and illustrator based in the North East of England. Her poems have been published in a variety of magazines and anthologies, including *The Rialto, Iota Poetry, Obsessed With Pipework, Butcher's Dog, The Interpreter's House*, the *Black Light Engine Room Literary Review, Kind of a Hurricane Press, The Emergency Poet, Beautiful Dragons* and *The Emma Press*. She is also the founder of the online poetry site, *The Fat Damsel*.

Marianne Burton's *She Inserts the Key* (Seren) was shortlisted for the Forward Best First Collection Prize 2013. Her next collection is due out from Seren in 2018.

Tina Chang is the Poet Laureate of Brooklyn. The first woman named to this position, she was raised in New York City. She is the author of the poetry collections *Half-Lit Houses* and *Of Gods & Strangers* (Four Way Books) and co-editor of the anthology *Language for a New Century: Contemporary Poetry from the Middle East, Asia and Beyond* (W.W. Norton, 2008) along with Nathalie Handal and Ravi Shankar. Her poems have appeared in *American Poet, McSweeney's, Ploughshares, The New York Times* among others. Her work has also been anthologized in *Identity Lessons, Poetry Nation, Asian American Literature, Asian American Poetry: The Next Generation, From the Fishouse: An Anthology of Poems* and *Poetry 30: Poets in Their Thirties*. She has received awards from the Academy of American Poets, the Barbara Deming Memorial Fund, the Ludwig Vogelstein Foundation, the New York Foundation for the Arts, Poets & Writers, the Van Lier Foundation among others. She currently teaches poetry at Sarah Lawrence College and is an international faculty member at the City University at Hong Kong.

Becky Cherriman is a writer, workshop leader and performer based in Leeds. Published by *Mslexia, New Walk, Envoi, Mother's Milk, Bloodaxe, Well Versed* and in *Poets For Corbyn*, she was resident poet for Morley Literature Festival in 2013. Her first pamphlet *Echolocation*, on the theme of mothering, and her first collection *Empires of Clay* were published in 2016 by Mother's Milk and Cinnamon Press respectively. Becky co-wrote and performed in Haunt, a site-specific theatre commission for Imove based on the experiences of homeless people. She is lead artist for Altofts Lit Fest In A Day /react-text www.beckycherriman.com

Geraldine Clarkson's poems have appeared in UK and international journals including *The Poetry Review* and *Poetry* (Chicago), and her poems have been broadcast on BBC Radio 3. She has a chapbook, *Declare*, with Shearsman Books (2016), selected as a Poetry Book Society Pamphlet Choice, and her pamphlet, *Dora Incites the Sea-Scribbler to Lament*, was selected as a Laureate's Choice (smith I doorstop, 2016). With Arts Council England support, she is preparing her first full-length collection.

Rose Cook is a well-known South West poet. She is an Apples & Snakes poet and co-founded the popular Devon poetry and performance forum One Night Stanza, as well as poetry performance group Dangerous Cardigans. Her latest book *Notes From a Bright Field* was published by Cultured Llama (2013). *www.rosecook.wordpress.com*
www.poems4peace.wordpress.com

Anna Crowe is co-founder and former Artistic Director of StAnza, Scotland's Poetry Festival. Her poetry includes two Peterloo collections and three Mariscat chapbooks, and has been translated into several languages. Awards include the Peterloo Poetry Prize, a Travelling Scholarship from the Society of Authors, the Callum Macdonald Memorial Award and two PBS Choices. Arc has published her translations of *Six Catalan Poets; Peatlands*, by Mexican poet, Pedro Serrano; and *Lunarium*, by Mallorcan poet, Josep Lluís Aguiló. *Love is a Place*, a third book of translations of poems by the Catalan poet, Joan Margarit, was published by Bloodaxe in 2016.

Julia Darling (b.1956; d.2005) worked as a community arts worker before taking up writing full-time in 1987. In 1988 her novel *Crocodile Soup* was long-listed for the Orange Prize, and a later novel, *The Taxi Driver's Daughter*, was long-listed for the Man Booker Prize and shortlisted for the Encore Award. In 2003, Julia was awarded the Northern Rock Foundation Writer's Award. Originally diagnosed with cancer at the age of 38, the disease initially went into remission but returned five years later. She used her writing as a means of conceptualising and dealing with illness: *Sudden Collapses in Public Places*, which received a Poetry Book Society recommendation, and her play, *Eating the Elephant*, which won three awards. In 2015, New Writing North and Julia's friends and family founded the Julia Darling Travel Fellowship, which commemorates Julia's work, and also her kind and generous spirit: http://juliadarling.co.uk.

Emma Donoghue was born in Dublin in 1969 and is an Irish emigrant twice over: she spent eight years in Cambridge doing a PhD in eighteenth-century literature before moving to London, Ontario, where she lives with her partner and their two children. She also migrates between genres, writing literary history, biography, stage and radio plays as well as short stories. She is best known for her novels, which range from the historical (*Frog Music, Slammerkin, Life Mask, Landing, The Sealed Letter*) to the contemporary (*Stir-Fry, Hood, Landing*). Her international bestseller *Room* was a finalist for the Man Booker, Commonwealth, and Orange Prizes and the film won her an Oscar nomination for Best Adapted Screenplay.

Christy Ducker is a Northumbrian poet, whose latest pamphlet, *Messenger* will be published in 2017. Her collection, *Skipper* (2015) includes work commended by the Forward Prize judges, and her pamphlet, *Armour* (2011) was a PBS Pamphlet Choice. Her commissions include work for Port of Tyne, English Heritage and York's Centre for Immunology and Infection. She directs the North East Heroes project, and is also a research fellow with Newcastle University's Institute for Creative Arts Practice. Christy began writing the day after the birth of her first child.

Dame Carol Ann Duffy DBE FRSL (b.1955) is a Scottish poet and playwright. She is Professor of Contemporary Poetry at Manchester Metropolitan University, and was appointed Britain's Poet Laureate in May 2009. She is the first woman, the first Scot, and the first openly LGBT person to hold the position. Her collections include *Standing Female Nude* (1985), winner of a Scottish Arts Council Award; *Selling Manhattan* (1987), which won a Somerset Maugham Award; *Mean Time* (1993), which won the Whitbread Poetry Award; and *Rapture* (2005), winner of the T.S. Eliot Prize. Her poems address issues such as oppression, gender, and violence in an accessible language that has made them popular in schools.

Sasha Dugdale is a poet, playwright, and translator and was born in Sussex, England. She has worked as a consultant for theatre companies in addition to writing her own plays. From 1995 to 2000, she worked for the British Council in Russia. She is author of the poetry collections *The Estate* (2007), *Notebook* (2003), and *Red House* (2011) and has translated Russian poetry and drama, including Anton Chekhov's *The Cherry Orchard*.

Helen Dunmore is a poet, novelist, short story and children's writer. Her poetry books have been given the Poetry Book Society Choice and Recommendations, Cardiff International Poetry Prize, Alice Hunt Bartlett Award and Signal Poetry Award, and *Bestiary* was shortlisted for the T.S. Eliot Prize. Her poem 'The Malarkey' won the 2010 National Poetry Competition. Her latest Bloodaxe poetry titles are *The Malarkey* (2012) and *Inside the Wave* (out in April 2017). She has published twelve novels and three books of short stories with Penguin, including *A Spell of Winter* (1995), winner of the Orange Prize for Fiction *Talking to the Dead* (1996), *The Siege* (2001), *Mourning Ruby* (2003), *House of Orphans* (2006) and *The Betrayal* (2010), as well as *The Greatcoat* (2012) with Hammer, and *The Lie* (2014) and *Exposure* (2016) with Hutchinson. She is a Fellow of the Royal Society of Literature and lives in Bristol.

Lily Dunn is an author and journalist. Her debut novel, *Shadowing the Sun*, was published to acclaim by Portobello Books. It was reviewed widely, and *The Sunday Times* called it an 'impressive and confident first novel'. Her journalism has featured in *Time Out, The Guardian, The Independent* and *Mail on Sunday*. She is currently studying for a PhD and writing Creative Nonfiction, some of which has been published by Granta. She has recently finished her second novel, *The Last Wave*.

Rhian Edwards is a multi-award winning poet. Her first collection *Clueless Dogs* (Seren) won Wales Book of the Year, the Roland Mathias Prize, Wales Book of the Year People's Choice, and was also shortlisted for the Forward Prize for Best First Collection. Her pamphlet *Parade the Fib* (Tall-Lighthouse) was awarded the Poetry Book Society Choice for Autumn 2008. She is the current winner of the John Tripp Award for Spoken Poetry, winning both the Judges and Audience award, and the first Writer in Residence at Aberystwyth Arts Centre from March to June 2013. Rhian's subsequent pamphlet *Brood* is due to be published in March 2017.

Nuala Ellwood moved to London in her twenties to pursue a career as a singer-songwriter, but ended up writing novels instead. She comes from a family of journalists, and they inspired her to get Arts Council funding to research and write a novel dealing with psychological trauma in the industry. Her debut thriller, *My Sister's Bones*, will be published by Penguin in February, 2017.

Carrie Etter is originally from Normal, Illinois, but has lived in England since 2001 and taught at Bath Spa University since 2004, where she is a Reader in Creative Writing. She has published three collections of poetry, most recently *Imagined Sons* (Seren, 2014), shortlisted for the Ted Hughes Award for New Work in Poetry. Additionally, she edited the anthology *Infinite Difference: Other Poetries by UK Women Poets* (Shearsman, 2010) and Linda Lamus's posthumous collection, *A Crater the Size of Calcutta* (Mulfran, 2015). She also publishes short stories, reviews and the occasional essay.

Suzanna Fitzpatrick has been widely published in magazines and anthologies, and has been commended in a number of competitions, won second prize in the 2010 Buxton Competition, and won the 2014 Hamish Canham Prize. Her poetry has also been aired on Radio 4, and her debut pamphlet, *Fledglings*, is published by Red Squirrel Press. She lives in Kent with her husband, son and daughter.

Carrie Fountain's poems have appeared in *American Poetry Review*, *Poetry*, and *Tin House*, among others. She is the author of the collections *Burn Lake* (Penguin, 2010) and *Instant Winner* (Penguin, 2014), and a recipient of the National Poetry Series Award. A former fellow at the Michener Center for Writers at the University of Texas, she is now writer-in-residence at St. Edward's University. Her first novel, *I'm Not Missing*, is forthcoming from Flatiron Books.

Tess Gallagher (b. 1943) is an American poet, essayist, novelist, and playwright. Her first collection of poems, *Instructions to the Double*, won the 1976 Elliston Book Award for 'best book of poetry published by a small press'. In 1984, she published the collection *Willingly*, which consists of poems written to and about her third husband, author Raymond Carver, who died in 1988. Other collections include *Dear Ghosts* (Graywolf Press, 2006); *My Black Horse: New and Selected Poems* (1995); *Owl-Spirit Dwelling* (1994) and *Moon Crossing Bridge* (1992). Her honours include a fellowship from the Guggenheim Foundation, two National Endowment of the Arts Awards, and the Maxine Cushing Gray Foundation Award.

Rebecca Goss's first collection *The Anatomy of Structures* was published by Flambard Press in 2010. Her second collection, *Her Birth* (Carcanet / Northern House), was shortlisted for The 2013 Forward Prize for Best Collection, The Warwick Prize for Writing 2015 and The Portico Prize for Literature 2015. In 2014 Rebecca was selected for The Poetry Book Society's Next Generation Poets.

Catherine Graham grew up in Newcastle-upon-Tyne where she still lives. Her first full collection, *Things I Will Put In My Mother's Pocket*, is published by Indigo Dreams Publishing. Catherine's latest collection, a pamphlet, *Like A Fish Out Of Batter: Poems after L. S. Lowry* is also published by IDP.

Kate Hendry is a writer, teacher and editor living in Edinburgh. Her first collection of poems, *The Lost Original*, was published by HappenStance Press in 2016. She runs reading groups for the Scottish Poetry Library and recently co-edited their anthology *Tools of the Trade: poems for new doctors*.

Rita Ann Higgins was born in 1955 in Galway, where she still lives. She left school at 14, and was in her late twenties when she started writing poetry. She has since published ten books of poetry, including *Sunny Side Plucked* (Poetry Book Society Recommendation) (1996), *An Awful Racket* (2001), *Throw in the Vowels: New & Selected Poems* (2005), *Ireland Is Changing Mother* (2011) and *Tongulish* (2016) from Bloodaxe, and *Hurting God: Prose & Poems* (2010) from Salmon. A celebrated playwright, her many awards include a Peadar O'Donnell Award in 1989 and several Arts Council bursaries, and she is a member of Aosdána.

Julie Hogg is a north-east poet and playwright with an MA in Creative Writing from the University of Teesside. Published in magazines and anthologies, her first pamphlet collection, *Majuba Road*, is available from Vane Women Press.

Laura Kasischke (pronounced Ka-ZISS-kee) was raised in Grand Rapids, Michigan. She is the recipient of the National Book Critics Circle Award for Poetry, 2012. She has published nine novels, three of which have been made into feature films – *The Life Before Her Eyes, Suspicious River, White Bird in a Blizzard* – and eight books of poetry, most recently *Space, in Chains*. Her new poetry collection, *The Infinitesimals*, was published in May, 2014. She has also published the short story collection, *If a Stranger Approaches You*. She has received fellowships from the Guggenheim Foundation, the National Endowment for the Arts, as well as several Pushcart Prizes and numerous awards. She is Allan Seager Collegiate Professor of English Language & Literature at the University of Michigan.

Melissa Lee-Houghton is a poet, fiction writer and essayist. Her short fiction has been broadcast on BBC Radio Four and she was awarded a Northern Writers' Award for her short fiction in 2016. A poem from her collection, *Sunshine* (Penned in the Margins, 2016), 'i am very precious', was shortlisted for the 2016 Forward Prize for Best Single Poem.

Pippa Little has a new collection, *Twist*, forthcoming. A chapbook, *Our Lady of Iguanas*, came out from the Black Light Engine Room Press in 2016. She is a Royal Literary Fund Fellow at Newcastle University.

Kate Long is the author of eight novels. Her first, *The Bad Mother's Handbook*, was a number one bestseller, was serialised on Radio 4, nominated for a British Book Award and turned into an ITV drama/DVD starring Catherine Tate. She has since written seven more novels: *Swallowing Grandma, Queen Mum, The Daughter Game, Mothers and Daughters, Before She Was Mine, Bad Mothers United* (the sequel to The Bad Mother's Handbook), and *Something Only We Know*. Kate's stories tend to focus on family drama and relationships between the generations, and her earlier work was heavily influenced by her Lancashire upbringing. www.katelongbooks.com

Emma McKervey is a Northern Irish poet whose work has appeared in many anthologies and journals including *The Compass Magazine* and *The Emma Press Anthology of Urban Myths and Legends*. She was recently short-listed in the Irish Book Awards for her poem 'Patagonia' as Irish poem of the year 2016.

Jane McKie's first two collections of poetry were *Morocco Rococo* (Cinnamon Press), which won the Sundial/Scottish Arts Council award for best first book of 2007, and *When the Sun Turns Green* (Polygon, 2009). In 2011, Jane won the Edwin Morgan poetry prize and published a pamphlet, *Garden of Bedsteads*, with Mariscat Press, a PBS Choice. Her most recent collection is *Kitsune* (Cinnamon Press, 2015). She is a Lecturer in Creative Writing at the University of Edinburgh.

Hollie McNish is a UK poet based between Glasgow and Cambridge. She has garnered titles like 'boundary breaker' (*Marie Claire*) and poet Benjamin Zephaniah stated 'I can't take my ears off her'. Her album *Versus* made her the first poet to record at Abbey Road Studios, London and her second collection of poems, *Cherry Pie*, was released by Burning Eye Books in 2015. *Nobody Told Me*, her latest memoir on parenthood, was released in February 2016 with Blackfriars to 5-star praise and *The Scotsman* stating, 'the world needs this book'.

Kathryn Maris is originally from New York and has lived in London since 1999. She has won a Pushcart Prize, an Academy of American Poets award and fellowships from the Fine Arts Work Center in Provincetown and Yaddo. She lives in London, where she teaches creative writing and writes essays and reviews. Her books include *God Loves You* (Seren, 2013) and *The Book of Jobs* (Four Way Books, 2006).

Hilary Menos was born in Luton in 1964, studied PPE at Wadham College, Oxford, and has an MA in Poetry from MMU. She has worked as a student union activist, journalist, food critic, and dramaturge. Her first collection, *Berg* (Seren, 2009) won the Forward Prize for Best First Collection. From 2004 to 2011 she co-ran an organic farm breeding Red Devon cattle and Wiltshire Horn sheep. Her second collection, *Red Devon*, was published by Seren in 2013. She has four children and lives in France. www.hilarymenos.co.uk

Esther Morgan was born in Kidderminster, Worcestershire. After completing an MA in Creative Writing at the University of East Anglia in

1997, she spent ten years as a freelance teacher and editor. Her three collections are all published by Bloodaxe. The most recent, *Grace* (2011), was shortlisted for the T.S. Eliot prize. Her fourth collection, *The Wound Register*, is due from Bloodaxe in spring 2018. She currently lives in Norfolk with her family.

Sinéad Morrissey (b. 1972) is the author of five collections of poetry, the last four of which have been shortlisted for the T.S. Eliot Award. Her most recent, *Parallax*, won the coveted prize in 2013. Her work has received numerous accolades including the Patrick Kavanagh Award (of which she was the youngest ever winner), the Michael Hartnett Prize and the *Irish Times*/Poetry Now Award. In 2007 she took first prize in the National Poetry Competition with 'Through the Square Window'. She is currently Professor in Creative Writing at the Seamus Heaney Centre for Poetry at Queen's University, Belfast.

Sarah Moss is a novelist, travel writer and academic, teaching in the University of Warwick's Writing Programme. Her latest novel, *The Tidal Zone* (Granta, 2016), was one of the winners in the Fiction Uncovered promotion for 2011, and was the Mumsnet Book of the Month for May 2012. Other novels include *Signs for Lost Children* (Granta, 2015), *Bodies of Light* (Granta, 2014), *Night Waking* (Granta, 2011) and *Cold Earth* (Granta, 2009). *Signs for Lost Children* and *Bodies of Light* were both shortlisted for the Wellcome Book Prize, in 2016 and 2015 respectively. Her non-fiction includes *Names for the Sea: Strangers in Iceland* (Granta, 2012) about living in Reykjavik in 2009–10, and academic books on Romantic-era British literature, food history and gender.

Ishbel Myerscough studied at Glasgow School of Art from 1987–91. After graduating she painted in a studio in Glasgow for two years, before going on to the Slade School of Art to do a postgraduate in 1993. At the end of her studies Ishbel was awarded a travel scholarship to New York. On returning to England she had her second exhibition with Anthony Mould, then travelled back to the USA, invited by Robert and Susan Summers to paint in their studios on their artists programme in Connecticut. Finally Ishbel settled in London and has lived and worked here since. She won the National Portrait Gallery BP Portrait Award in 1995, and has since completed two portrait commissions for their collection. Her painting 'Mothers and Daughters' appears on the cover of this book.

Marie Naughton's poems have appeared in magazines and anthologies in the UK and Ireland including *Mslexia, The Dark Horse, Southword, The Stony Thursday Book, Lines Underwater* and *Her Wings of Glass*. She won the

Cafe Writers competition in 2012 and was shortlisted for the Flambard Poetry Prize in 2015 and the Basil Bunting Prize in 2016. She has an MA in Creative Writing from the Centre for New Writing at Manchester University. She is a psychotherapist and lives in Manchester.

Nuala Ní Chonchúir was born in Dublin, Ireland, she lives in East Galway. She has published four short story collections, the most recent *Mother America* appeared from New Island in 2012. A chapbook of short-short stories *Of Dublin and Other Fictions* appeared from Tower Press in the US in 2013. Her third collection *The Juno Charm* was published in 2011 and her critically acclaimed second novel *The Closet of Savage Mementos* was shortlisted for the Kerry Irish Novel of the Year Award 2015. Published under Nuala O'Connor, her third novel, *Miss Emily*, about the poet Emily Dickinson and her Irish maid, was shortlisted for the Bord Gáis Energy Eason Book Club Novel of the Year and longlisted for the MM Bennetts Award for Historical Fiction. www.nualanichonchuir.com

Doireann Ní Ghríofa is a bilingual writer from Ireland. She was recipient of the Ireland Chair of Poetry Bursary 2015 and the Rooney Prize for Irish Literature 2016. Her third book *Clasp* was shortlisted for the Irish Times Poetry Award 2016 and was awarded the Michael Hartnett Poetry Prize.

Sharon Olds (b.1942) is one of contemporary poetry's leading voices. Winner of several prestigious awards, including fellowships from the Guggenheim Foundation and the National Endowment for the Arts, the Pulitzer Prize, the T.S. Eliot Prize, the Wallace Stevens Award, and National Book Critics Circle Award, Olds is known for writing intensely personal, emotionally scathing poetry which graphically depicts family life as well as global political events. Widely anthologized, her work has also been published in a number of journals and magazines. She was New York State Poet from 1998 to 2000, and teaches on the writing programme at New York University. Her latest collection is *Odes* (Jonathan Cape, 2016).

Alicia Ostriker is a poet and critic, twice finalist for the National Book Award. Her most recent poetry collection is *the Old Woman, the Tulip, and the Dog* (University of Pittsburgh Press, 2014). As a critic she is the author of *Stealing the Language: the Emergence of Women's Poetry in America* (Beacon Press, 1986) and other books on poetry and on the Bible.

Alice Oswald's first collection of poetry, *The Thing in the Gap-Stone Stile* (1996), received a Forward Poetry Prize for Best First Collection. Oswald's other collections of poetry include *Dart* (2002), *Woods, etc.*

(2005), winner of a Geoffrey Faber Memorial Prize; *Weeds and Wild Flowers* (2009), illustrated by Jessica Greenman; *A Sleepwalk on the Severn* (2009); and *Memorial* (2011), a reworking of Homer's *Iliad* that has received high critical praise for its innovative approach and stunning imagery, which won the 2013 Warwick Prize for writing. Oswald's many honours and awards include an Eric Gregory Award, an Arts Foundation Award for Poetry, a Forward Prize for Best Single Poem, and a Ted Hughes Award.

Ellen Phethean's first poetry collection *Breath* (Flambard, 2009) was shortlisted for the London New Poetry Award 2010. Her second collection, *Portrait of the Quince as an Older Woman* (Red Squirrel Press, 2014), was a New Writing North Read Regional Choice for 2014. She's written a young adult novel, *Ren and the Blue Hands*, published Nov 2016 by Red Squirrel Press. www.diamondtwig.co.uk Twitter @phethean

Stav Poleg's poetry has appeared in *The New Yorker*, *Poetry London* and *Poetry Ireland Review* among others. Her graphic-novel piece 'Dear Penelope: Variations on an August Morning,' with artist Laura Gressani, was acquired by the Scottish National Gallery of Modern Art. She lives in Cambridge.

Clare Pollard's new translation of *Ovid's Heroines* (Bloodaxe, 2013) has recently toured as a one-woman show with Jaybird Live Literature. Her fifth collection, about motherhood, is *Incarnation* (Bloodaxe, 2017). Her website is www.clarepollard.com

Clare Potter is a writer, performer and educator from Cefn Fforest, Wales. She spent ten years in the Deep South where she did an MA in Afro-Caribbean literature. She teaches creative writing at Cardiff University and won the John Tripp Award for Spoken Poetry. Her work has been published in *Planet*, *New Welsh Review*, *Wales Arts Review*, *Mslexia*, *Cahoots Magazine*, *Cambrensis*, *The Seminary Ridge Review* and various anthologies. Her first poetry collection is *spilling histories*. She has written for the Welsh National Opera in community theatre and singing projects, and has received various commissions to write poetry in collaboration with artists.

Wendy Pratt lives and works in Filey, North Yorkshire. She has enjoyed publication of her poetry in many journals and magazines and has published three collections of poetry. *Nan Hardwick Turns into a Hare* and her first full collection, *Museum Pieces*, were both published by *Prolebooks*. Her latest pamphlet, *Lapstrake*, is published by *Flarestack Poets*. She is currently completing a PhD at Hull University and is poetry correspondent for *Northern Soul*.

Mel Pryor grew up in Hong Kong and London and trained as a solicitor. She has won the Philip Larkin Poetry Prize and the Ware Sonnet Prize. Her pamphlet, *Drawn on Water*, was published in 2014 and her first full collection, *Small Nuclear Family*, in 2015, both by Eyewear. The *TLS* described *Small Nuclear Family* as 'a remarkable debut'.

Deryn Rees-Jones is a poet, editor and critic. She co-directs the Centre for New and International Writing at the University of Liverpool, where she is Professor of Poetry. Her Selected Poems, *What It's Like to Be Alive*, was recently published by Seren. She is currently writing a book on the work of the Portuguese artist Paula Rego.

Rachel Richardson is the author of two collections of poetry, *Hundred-Year Wave* and *Copperhead*. Her poems have been awarded the Wallace Stegner Fellowship and the National Endowment for the Arts Fellowship, and have appeared in the *PN Review*, the *New York Times*, and elsewhere. She teaches at various universities, parents two daughters, and co-directs the literary arts center Left Margin LIT in Berkeley, California.

Emma Simon has been published in various magazines, including *The Rialto, Interpreter's House* and *Bare Fiction*. She was selected for the Jerwood/Arvon Mentoring scheme in 2015, and her pamphlet *Dragonish* will be published by The Emma Press in 2017.

Jacqueline Saphra's pamphlet, *Rock'n'Roll Mamma* was published by Flarestack in 2008 and her first full collection, *The Kitchen of Lovely Contraptions* (flipped eye, 2011)) was developed with funding from Arts Council England and nominated for The Aldeburgh First Collection Prize. A book of illustrated prose poems, *If I Lay on my Back I saw Nothing but Naked Women*, was published by The Emma Press in November 2014. This was developed into a performance piece with music and won Best Collaborative Work at the Saboteur Awards 2015. *All My Mad Mothers*, her second full collection, will be out from Nine Arches Press in May 2017. She teaches at The Poetry School.

Rosie Sandler lives in Essex, where she writes and edits poems, stories and novels, and runs poetry workshops. Her poems have appeared in a number of journals and anthologies, including: *The Poetry of Sex* (Penguin Books, ed. Sophie Hannah), *The Rialto, Lighthouse Journal, Popshot Magazine* and *The Emma Press Anthology of Dance*. She was a featured reader in the 2014 Essex Poetry Festival. Rosie hosts 'The Poet's Resource' – a submissions blog for poets: https://thepoetsresource.wordpress.com https://rosiesandler.co.uk/

Brenda Shaughnessy is the author of four poetry collections, most recently *So Much Synth* (2016, Copper Canyon Press) and *Our Andromeda* (2012), which was a finalist for the Kingsley Tufts Award, The International Griffin Prize, the PEN Open Book Award, and was one of *The New York Times'* 2013 Notable Books. Her work has appeared in *Best American Poetry, Harpers, The New York Times, The New Yorker, O* Magazine, *Paris Review, Poetry* Magazine, and elsewhere. A 2013 Guggenheim Foundation Fellow, she is Associate Professor of English and Creative Writing at Rutgers University-Newark. She lives in Verona, NJ with her family.

Natalie Shaw lives and works in London, with children of varying ages and a kind husband. Her poetry appears in numerous print and online journals and anthologies, most recently *Schooldays* (Paper Swans) and *The Very Best of 52* (Nine Arches Press). Twitter @redbaronski

Kathryn Simmonds has published two books of poetry *Sunday at the Skin Launderette* (2008) and *The Visitations* (2013), and a novel, *Love and Fallout* (2014) all with Seren. In 2013/14 she was poet-in-residence at The Charles Causley Trust in Cornwall. She lives in Norwich with her husband and two young daughters and teaches for The Poetry School.

Ruth Stacey's debut poetry collection, *Queen, Jewel, Mistress*, was published by Eyewear in July 2015. Her pamphlet, *Fox Boy*, was published by Dancing Girl Press in 2014. She works as a lecturer in creative writing and is currently editing her second full poetry collection. She lives in Worcestershire. www.ruthstacey.com

Greta Stoddart was born in Oxfordshire. Her first collection *At Home in the Dark* (Anvil) was shortlisted for the Forward Prize for Best First Collection and won the Geoffrey Faber Memorial Prize in 2002. Her second book, *Salvation Jane*, was shortlisted for the Costa Book Award 2008. She was also shortlisted for the Forward Prize for Best Individual Poem in 2012. Her third book, *Alive Alive O* (Bloodaxe, 2015), was shortlisted for the Roehampton Poetry Prize 2016. She lives in Devon and teaches for the Poetry School and the Arvon Foundation.

Degna Stone is a poet, editor and producer based in Tyne and Wear. She is a co-founder of *Butcher's Dog* poetry magazine, and is currently a fellow of The Complete Works III. She is also an Inscribe-supported writer, holds an MA in Creative Writing from Newcastle University, and she received a Northern Writers Award in 2015.

Rebecca Stonehill is an author and teacher of creative writing to young people. She created Magic Pencil, an initiative that gives greater exposure to creative writing, poetry and storytelling to those who otherwise may not have access to it. She has written two novels, published by Bookouture, *The Poet's Wife* and *The Girl and the Sunbird*. Rebecca currently lives in Nairobi with her husband and three children. You can read more about her work through her website and blog www.rebeccastone-hill.com

Agnieszka Studzinska has an MA in Creative Writing from the UEA. Her first collection, *Snow Calling*, was shortlisted for the London New Poetry Award 2010. Her second collection, *What Things Are* is described by the award winning novelist and poet, Michael Symmons Roberts, as a 'A subtle and beautiful collection in which – poem by poem – the possibility of true knowledge is tested. Intimate and attentive, each poem returns to the question of what we can know of the world and each other.' She is currently working on her PhD at Royal Holloway.

C.L. Taylor is the one of the biggest stars of psychological thriller fiction. She is the bestselling author of *The Accident*, *The Lie* and *The Missing*, which have sold almost a million copies in the UK to date. She writes full time and lives in Bristol with her partner and young son.

Wendy Videlock lives on the western slope of the Colorado Rockies. Her work has appeared in *Best American Poetry*, *Hudson Review*, *Poetry Magazine*, *The New Criterion*, and other literary journals. Her books, *Nevertheless*, *The Dark Gnu*, and *Slingshots*, are available from Able Muse Press.

Jackie Wills has published five collections of poetry: *Woman's Head as Jug* (Arc, 2013), *Commandments* (Arc, 2007), *Fever Tree* (Arc, 2003), *Party* (Leviathan, 2000), *Powder Tower* (Arc, 1995) and a pamphlet, *Black Slingbacks* (Slow Dancer, 1992). She was shortlisted for the 1995 T.S. Eliot prize and in 2004 was one of *Mslexia* magazine's 10 new women poets of the decade. She trained as a journalist and has earned her living as a writer since 1978.

Karen McCarthy Woolf was born in London to English and Jamaican parents. She has been awarded residencies at the literary development agency Spread the Word, the City of El Gouna, Egypt and at the National Maritime Museum in Greenwich in 2015 where she responded to an exhibit on migration. Having read at a wide variety of national and international venues and festivals, including Cheltenham, Aldeburgh, Ledbury, the Royal Festival Hall, Barbican Centre, V&A, Tate Modern and Science Museum in the UK, as well as in the US, Singapore, Sweden and the Caribbean, she is known as a compelling presenter of her work.

Her poetry collection, *An Aviary of Small Birds* – a book of elegies that commemorates a stillborn son (Carcanet, 2014) – was a Poetry Book Society Recommendation, a *Guardian/Observer* book of the month, and was nominated for both the Forward and Aldeburgh Best First Collection Prizes.

Jo Young is an Army veteran and mum to two young boys. She has been writing since she left the Regular Army in 2014 and is a doctoral student on the University of Glasgow's Creative Writing DFA programme.

Rachel Zucker is the author of nine books, most recently, a memoir, *MOTHERs*, and a double collection of prose and poetry, *The Pedestrians*. Her book *Museum of Accidents* was a finalist for the National Book Critics Circle Award. She received a National Endowment for the Arts Fellowship in 2013. Zucker teaches poetry at New York University and is currently delivering a series of lectures on the intersection of poetry, confession, ethics and disobedience as part of the Bagley Wright Lecture Series. @rachzuck www.rachelzucker.net

ACKNOWLEDGEMENTS

Thanks are due to the editors of those publications in which work reprinted here first appeared: Patricia Ace, 'First Blood', originally published in *Fabulous Beasts* (Freight Books, 2013); Louisa Adjoa Parker, 'His Khakia Hood', printed here with permission of the author; Natalya Anderson 'The Woman in Clericals', originally published by *And Other Poems*; Mary Austin Speaker, 'After the First Child, the Second', originally published by the Academy of American Poets' Poem-A-Day program; Janette Ayachi, 'Plasticine Love Hearts', printed here by permission of the author; Anna Barker, 'The Writer Me and the Mother Me', printed here by permission of the author; Elizabeth Barrett, 'Good things happened that day also', originally published by *And Other Poems*, https://andotherpoems.com; interview with Teika Bellamy printed with permission of Teika Bellamy; Deborah J. Bennett, 'Laundry', originally published in Salamander Magazine, issue 41; Fiona Benson, 'Eurofighter Typhoon', originally published in *Poetry London*, issue 86, Autumn 2016; Kaddy Benyon, 'Strange Fruit', originally published in *Milk Fever* (Salt, 2012); Zoë Brigley, 'Motherhood is Valuable for the Creative Life', originally published at http://zoëbrigley.com; Liz Berry, 'Connemara', originally published by *And Other Poems*, https://andotherpoems.com; Kate Bingham, 'The World at One', originally published in *The New Statesman*, 28 Feb 2016; Sujata Bhatt, '29 April 1989', originally published in *Collected Poems*, (Carcanet, 2013); Jane Burn, printed here by permission of the author; Marianne Burton, 'Meditation on the Hours: 5pm: The Lie of the Pool', originally published in *She Inserts the Key* (Seren, 2013); Tina Chang, 'Milk', published here by permission of the author; Becky Cherriman, 'The Foster Mother's Blanket', originally published in *Echolocation* (Mother's Milk Books, 2016); Geraldine Clarkson, 'Monica's Overcoat of Flesh', originally published in *Poetry London*, Issue 77, Spring 2015; Rose Cook, 'Poem for Someone who is Juggling Her Life', originally published in *Notes from a Bright Field* (Cultured Llama, 2012); Anna Crowe, 'Amniotic', published here by permission of the author; Julia Darling, 'Advice for My Daughters', originally published in *Indelible, Miraculous* (Arc, 2015), reprinted re-printed with kind permission from Julia Darling's family; interview with Emma Donoghue printed with permission of Emma Donoghue; Christy Ducker, 'And', originally published in *Skipper* (Poetry Business, 2015); Carol Ann Duffy's 'Water' originally published in *The Bees* (Picador, 2011); Sasha Dugdale, 'Lifting the bedcovers and there', originally published in *Red House* (Carcanet/Oxford Poets, 2011); Helen Dunmore, 'Domestic Poem', originally published in *The Apple Fall* (Bloodaxe Books, 1983); Lily Dunn, 'The Mutable Bed', printed here

First Week', from 'The Wellspring', published by Jonathan Cape. Reproduced by permission of The Random House Group Ltd; Alicia Ostriker, 'Paragraphs', originally published in *The Mother/Child Papers* (Beacon Press, 1980); Alice Oswald, 'Poem for Carrying a Baby Out of Hospital', originally published in *Woods, etc.* (Faber, 2005); Ellen Phethean, 'Youngest Son Leaves Home', *Portrait of the Quince as an Older Woman* (Red Squirrel Press, 2015); Stav Poleg, 'At the Gallery of Modern Art', printed here by permission of the author; Wendy Pratt, 'Sixth Birthday', printed here by permission of the author; Clare Pollard, 'The Reef', originally published in *Poetry Spotlight*, 29 Oct 2016; Clare Potter, 'Self-Soothing' printed here with permission of the author; Mel Pryor, originally published in *Small Nuclear Family* (Eyewear Press, 2015); Deryn Rees-Jones, 'Afterthought', originally published in *Quiver* (Seren, 2004); Rachel Richardson, 'Transmission', originally published in *Hundred-Year Wave*, reprinted with the permission of The Permissions Company, Inc., on behalf of Carnegie Mellon University Press, www.cmu.edu/universitypress; Emma Simon, 'Plait', originally published by *And Other Poems*; Jacqueline Saphra, 'What Time is it in Nova Scotia?' originally published in *Ambit 225* (2016); Rosie Sandler, 'Maternal Instincts', reprinted here by permission of the author; Brenda Shaughnessy, 'Magi', originally published in *Our Andromeda* (Copper Canyon Press, 2012); Natalie Shaw, 'How to Tell Your Son He Has No Friends', originally published by *And Other Poems*; Kathryn Simmonds, 'Memorial', printed here by permission of the author; Ruth Stacey, 'On a Cautious Road', originally published by *Ink, Sweat, and Tears*, http://www.inksweatandtears.co.uk; Greta Stoddart, 'At the School Gates', originally published in *Salvation Jane* (Anvil, 2008); Degna Stone, 'Ruby, aged 4½', originally published in *Butcher's Dog*, issue 1, Autumn 2012; Rebecca Stonehill; 'Writer and Mother: How Children Can Help (and Not Hinder) the Creative Process', printed with permission of the author; Agnieszka Studzinska, 'Boat', originally published in *What Things Are* (Eyewear, 2014); CL Taylor, 'How Motherhood Turned me to Crime', printed here with permission of the author; Wendy Videlock, 'Flowers', originally published in *POETRY*, Feb 2012; Jackie Wills, 'Giya's Maps', originally published in *Fever Tree* (Arc, 2003); Karen McCarthy Woolf, 'White Butterflies', originally published in *An Aviary of Small Birds* (Carcanet, 2014); Jo Young, 'The Lady Standard-Bearer from the British Legion', printed here with permission of the author; Rachel Zucker, 'The Day I Lost My Déjà Vu', first published in Museum of Accidents, Wave Books, (2009).

THANKS

To Claire Malcolm at New Writing North, for support and inspiration above and beyond; to Debbie Taylor and all the team at *Mslexia* for hosting the blog.

To Arts Council England for funding the Writing Motherhood tour throughout 2014–15. To Matt Holland at Swindon Festival of Literature; to Susie Troup at Hexham Book Festival; to Beverly Ward, Liz Rosenberg, Marilyn Taylor, Vicky Allen, Ruth Stacey, Helen Cadbury, and Steph Vidal-Hall for chairing events; Eleanor Livingstone at StAnza Poetry Festival; Rebecca Wilkie at Durham Book Festival; Abigail Campbell and Jonathan Davidson at Birmingham Literature Festival; York Literature Festival; Adrian Turpin and Anne Barclay at Wigtown Book Festival; Keith Acheson at Belfast Book Festival; Maria de Souza at Off the Shelf Festival of Words (Sheffield); Jo Furber at the Dylan Thomas Centre (Swansea); Vic Arscott at Ledbury Poetry Festival; Andrew Forster at the Wordsworth Trust; Lionel Ward at Taunton Literary Festival; and to all who performed at and attended the events. A special shout out to Kathryn Maris, C.L. Taylor, and Nuala Ellwood for friendship and support.

To Amy Wack and Mick Felton for their enthusiasm for this anthology, and to all the contributors; to Jared Jess-Cooke for love, support, encouragement, always finding my keys, making me laugh, and naps. To our children, Melody, Phoenix, Summer, and Willow, for changing everything for the better.

EDITOR NOTE

Carolyn Jess-Cooke (b. 1978) is a writer, editor, and academic from Belfast, Northern Ireland. Her poetry collection *Inroads* (Seren, 2010) received an Eric Gregory Award from the Society of Authors, a Tyrone Guthrie Prize, a Northern Writers Award and a Major Arts Council of England Award, and was shortlisted for several others. Her second collection, *Boom!* (Seren, 2014), received a Northern Writers Award and a K Blundell Award from the Society of Authors. Her novels *The Guardian Angel's Journal* (Piatkus, 2011) and *The Boy Who Could See Demons* (Piatkus, 2012) are published in a total of 23 languages, and a third novel is forthcoming from HarperCollins (UK) in summer 2017. As Lecturer in Creative Writing at the University of Glasgow she leads research in the fields of creative writing and mental health and the impact of motherhood on women's writing. She lives with her husband and four children in north-east England.

SEREN
Well chosen words

Seren is an independent publisher with a wide-ranging list which includes poetry, fiction, biography, art, translation, criticism and history. Many of our books and authors have been on longlists and shortlists for – or won – major literary prizes, among them the Costa Award, the Jerwood Fiction Uncovered Prize, the Man Booker, the Desmond Elliott Prize, The Writers' Guild Award, Forward Prize and TS Eliot Prize.

At the heart of our list is a beautiful poem, a good story told well or an idea or history presented interestingly or provocatively. We're international in authorship and readership though our roots are here in Wales (Seren means Star in Welsh), where we prove that writers from a small country with an intricate culture have a worldwide relevance.

Our aim is to publish work of the highest literary and artistic merit that also succeeds commercially in a competitive, fast changing environment. You can help us achieve this goal by reading more of our books – available from all good bookshops and increasingly as e-books. You can also buy them at 20% discount from our website, and get monthly updates about forthcoming titles, readings, launches and other news about Seren and the authors we publish.

www.serenbooks.com